Constitutional Law in Poland

Constitutional Law in Poland

Second Edition

Agnieszka Bień-Kacała
Anna Młynarska-Sobaczewska

This book was originally published as a monograph in the International Encyclopaedia of Laws/Constitutional Law.

Founding Editor: Roger Blanpain
General Editor: Frank Hendrickx
Volume Editors: André Alen & David Haljan

Wolters Kluwer

Published by:
Kluwer Law International B.V.
PO Box 316
2400 AH Alphen aan den Rijn
The Netherlands
E-mail: international-sales@wolterskluwer.com
Website: lrus.wolterskluwer.com

Sold and distributed by:
Wolters Kluwer Legal & Regulatory U.S.
7201 McKinney Circle
Frederick, MD 21704
United States of America
Email: customer.service@wolterskluwer.com

ISBN 978-94-035-3300-1

e-Book: ISBN 978-94-035-3301-8
web-PDF: ISBN 978-94-035-3302-5

The Authors

Agnieszka Bień-Kacała is an Associate Professor of Constitutional Law at the Faculty of Law and Administration at Nicolaus Copernicus University in Toruń, Poland. Her research expertise covers liberal and illiberal constitutionalism, constitutional changes, Polish and comparative constitutional law. She provides expertise to the Marshal of the Polish Senate. Her new, co-edited (with Tímea Drinóczi) book *Rule of Law, Common Values, and Illiberal Constitutionalism: Poland and Hungary within the European Union* has been published by Routledge (2021).

Address:
Department of Constitutional Law
Faculty of Law and Administration
Nicolaus Copernicus University in Toruń, Poland
ORCID 0000-0002-9559-3130
abien@umk.pl
00 48 509 554 767
Uniwersytet Mikołaja Kopernika w Toruniu
Wydział Prawa i Administracji
ul. Bojarskiego 3
87-100 Torun
Poland

The Authors

Anna Młynarska-Sobaczewska has been working in the field of constitutional law. Since 2013, she has been affiliated with the Institute of Law Studies of the Polish Academy of Sciences and has been the Head of the Department of Constitutional Law and European Research since 2016. Her interest fields include theory of constitutional law (legitimacy of public authorities, constitutional adjudication, transitional states), constitutionalism and human rights, in particular freedom of press, freedom of artistic creativity, right to culture.

Address:
The Institute of Law Studies, Polish Academy of Sciences
Department of Constitutional Law and European Research
ORCID: 0000-0003-3029-2836
anka.sobaczewska@gmail.com
The Institute of Law Studies, Polish Academy of Sciences, Nowy Swiat 72, 00-330 Warsaw, Poland
Tel: 00 48 22 8267571
00 48 601268431

Table of Contents

List of Abbreviations

CHR Act	Act on the Commissioner for Human Rights
CJEU	Court of Justice of the European Union
CT	Constitutional Tribunal
EAW	European Arrest Warrant
ECHR	European Court of Human Rights
ENCJ	European Network of Councils for the Judiciary
EU	European Union
KRRiT	National Broadcasting Council
MP	Member of Parliament
NBP	National Bank of Poland
NCJ	National Council of the Judiciary
PAC	Provincial Administrative Court
PLN	Polish złoty
RP	Republic of Poland
SAC	Supreme Administrative Court
SAO	Supreme Audit Office
SC	Supreme Court
TEU	The Treaty on European Union
TS	Tribunal of State

List of Abbreviations

General Introduction

§1. Outline of Polish Constitutional History

1. The earliest days of Polish statehood are inseparably linked to the reign of Mieszko I (ca. AD 922–AD 992) and the baptism of Poland performed in accordance with the Latin rite in AD 966. Generally, during the time of the early feudal monarchy, rulers carried the title of duke, and only in exceptional circumstances did they manage to obtain the royal title (Bolesław I the Brave – 1025, Mieszko II – 1025 and Bolesław the Bold – 1076). The royal authority increased the prestige and position of the monarch both outside and inside the country. It reinforced the centralisation of the State. However, intensive decentralisation efforts led to fragmentation of Poland and increased prominence of local provinces. The reunification of the State was carried out by Władysław Łokietek (*the Short*), crowned in 1320. Therefore, from the very beginning, the Polish statehood was shaped in line with the unitarian trend. However, the later period saw a dynamic development of the Polish-Lithuanian Commonwealth, which by virtue of the Union of Lublin functioned as a complex (federal) state comprising the Crown of the Kingdom of Poland and the Grand Duchy of Lithuania between 1569 and 1795.

2. Apart from the monarch rule, the power of the nobility (Pol. *Szlachta*) (and then of Polish and Lithuanian magnates) gradually evolved, manifesting itself in the institutions of the dietines (also referred to as *district sejmiks*) and then the general Sejm. The first full or ordinary Sejm of the Crown was convened in 1493 in Piotrków. It consisted of three authorities: the King, the Senate (the former royal council, consisting of Catholic archbishops and bishops, voivodes, castellans and dignitaries of the Crown and Court) and the Chamber of Deputies (a representation of the nobility elected by the district sejmiks).

3. The principle of the King's election by the nobility played a particular role in the constitutional history of the Polish State. The tradition of the royal election in Poland dates back to 1572. The Election Sejm chose the monarch during the *interregnum* period.

4. Years later, constitutional monarchy started developing in Poland in the 1760s, when the reform of the State began introducing, among other things, limitation of the *liberum veto* right (the rule related to the unanimity of votes – a form of opposition to parliamentary resolutions that often led to cancellation of the session of the Sejm and nullification of its work) and writing down the principle of majority voting. The last King of Poland, Stanisław August Poniatowski, was elected in 1764.

5. Obviously, constitutions play the key role in constitutional history of every state. Fundamental laws remain the cornerstone of their development. The first Polish Constitution (also considered the first in Europe and the second worldwide) was passed on 3 May 1791. It contained modern political principles, such as sovereignty of the Nation (in fact including only the nobility) and the separation of powers. The political system defined in the Constitution of 3 May 1791 was described as a constitutional monarchy. Legislative power was entrusted to the Sejm and the Senate; executive power was given to the King, the Guardians of the Laws (modelled after the English cabinet of ministers) and the Grand and Order Committees; judicial power was exercised by the courts. This Constitution also introduced solutions that could be considered the original basis for today's mechanisms of political and constitutional accountability.

6. The enactment of the Constitution of 3 May 1791 and the state reforms it envisaged did not protect Poland from the abolition of statehood for the period of 123 years. Despite the reforms and efforts undertaken to maintain the State's integrity, the imperialist tendencies of the neighbours (Russia, Austria, Prussia) led to the partition of Poland in years: 1772, 1793 and 1795. In 1795, the Commonwealth of Poland was forced to end its independent existence and ceased to be a state.

7. Poland regained its independence in 1918 with the creation of the so-called Second Republic following the conclusion of World War I. When the war was coming to an end, the Regency Council was established and proclaimed the creation of a new, independent state. The Council then handed over full power to Józef Piłsudski. Piłsudski, acting as the Commander-in-Chief, and then as the Provisional Chief of State, undertook the task of organising the reconstituted State. The decree of 22 November 1918 defined the state system as a republic, and until the Legislative Sejm was formed, the Chief of State was entrusted with the highest authority. Then the work on the Polish Constitution began – at the same time, the struggle to establish and maintain the borders of Poland continued (the war with Bolshevik Russia, plebiscites concerning state affiliation in the western territories).

8. After Poland had regained its independence, the first constitution was passed on 17 March 1921 ('March Constitution'). The basic political principles were as follows: republican form of state, sovereignty of the nation and separation of powers. The Constitution entrusted the Sejm (lower chamber of Parliament) and the Senate with legislative power. The Deputies and Senators were elected by universal suffrage, and the Sejm and the Senate formed the National Assembly, which elected the President. The President, together with the Government, was considered to constitute the executive power. The members of the Government (the Prime Minister and ministers) were held politically (for conducting the Government's policy as Parliament, jointly and individually) and constitutionally (for violating the constitution and laws) accountable. Courts were appointed to administer justice. Due to the political fragmentation of the Parliament, the parliamentary system proved unstable and, as a consequence, the formation of the Government was hampered. Cabinet crises occurred quite frequently. That caused J. Piłsudski to carry out the so-called May Coup in 1926. As a result, both the Prime Minister and the President left their offices. The period of the so-called Sanation, i.e., repair of the State, began.

9. Revision of the political system was based on the amendment of the Constitution, the so-called August Novelization of 2 August 1926. In this document, the President was granted extraordinary powers. It turned out to be of key significance to grant the Head of State the power to issue statutory regulations and the option of dissolving the Parliament before the end of the term. The Sanation was also the time of repressions against the opposition, including numerous arrests. The actual power was held by J. Piłsudski, who also assumed the post of Head of Government but did not accept the presidential office despite being officially elected. The way of exercising power and the use of competencies by individual authorities follow the European trend in this respect. In order to protect themselves against totalitarian movements (Fascism, Nazism, Communism), European democracies showed tendencies towards militant democracy of an authoritarian nature.

10. Sanation in Poland strived to adopt a new constitution. It came into force on 23 April 1935 and introduced an authoritarian model of government, although it was not nationalistic in nature. The new Constitution was based on: identification of the State as a commonwealth of citizens with the State as a point of reference (according to the concept of solidarity, the individual was subordinated to the State and had the obligation to cooperate with the State for both the State and the common good), uniformity of state power (the separation of powers was abolished) and elitism. According to the new structure of power, the President represented a unified and indivisible power. His office was superior to the Sejm and the Senate, the Government, armed forces, courts and state scrutiny. The President did not bear any responsibility – according to the wording of the Constitution, he answered only 'before God and history'. The powers of the Head of State concerned the legislative, constitutional, executive, control and emergency issues in the time of war. This last element summarises the shape of the political system and the practice on the eve of World War II, which began on 1 September 1939 with the Nazi invasion of Poland. Nevertheless, the President's competency related to the possibility of appointing a successor in case of war made it possible to somehow continue the statehood in the form of an émigré centre of power until 1990, when the President of the Republic of Poland (RP) in exile, Ryszard Kaczorowski, handed over the presidential insignia to newly elected Lech Wałęsa.

11. The end of World War II resulted in the surrender of Poland to the influence of the Soviet Union and the communist regime. One of the first founding acts of the new system – people's democracy – is the Manifesto of the Polish Committee for National Liberation of 22 July 1944. It recognised the State National Council as the only legitimate authority, which was designed to perform the functions of Parliament. The March Constitution was indicated in the Manifesto as the basis for the operation of the state and public authorities. As a result of the popular referendum of 1946, the Senate was abolished and elections to the Legislative Sejm were held in 1947. This Sejm enacted an interim constitution, the so-called Small Constitution, based on the provisions of the March Constitution. This regulation envisaged the institution of the President. It was abolished when the Constitution of the Polish People's Republic was passed on 22 July 1952. This Constitution introduced a completely new political system of socialist states (people's democracy) inspired by the political solutions of the Soviet Union. Its foundations were: the republican form of state; the sovereignty of 'working people in towns and villages' (instead of *the People*); the socialist development of the state; the workers' and peasants' alliance; the leading role of the working class; the leading role of the Polish United Workers' Party and proletarian internationalism. The Constitution clearly rejected the separation of powers and assigned the position of the supreme bodies of state to the Sejm and the Council of State. The State of that period can be regarded as repressive. The highest form of repression against its own citizens was the imposition of martial law on 13 December 1981. The underlying reason was the desire to preserve the structures of power in their then form. Martial law was declared to have been introduced in a manner inconsistent with the then binding Constitution, regardless of its inconsistency with the Polish Constitution of 1997, as stated by the Constitutional Tribunal (hereinafter 'CT') on 16 March 2011 (K 35/08).

12. When that period was coming to an end, the socialist regime introduced bodies which, as a result of their activities, contributed to the disintegration of the political system of the People's Republic of Poland and led to formation of liberal democracy. These were: the Supreme Administrative Court (SAC) (1980), the CT (1982/1985) and the Ombudsman (1987).

13. The interim constitutions also played a significant role in the constitutional history of Poland. They regulated the most important systemic issues during the transformation period. Their task was to temporarily establish the principles of functioning of the State until the adoption of a comprehensive constitution, i.e., one that regulated all the State's political and governmental issues. Such legal acts had been in force since 1919, until the Constitution of 17 March 1921 came into force – the Small Constitution defined the system of the newly reborn state. The subsequent interim constitution was passed in 1947, when the foundations of the People's Republic of Poland were laid, and remained in force until 1952, when the Constitution of the People's Republic of Poland was adopted.

14. The period of political transformation and the transition from a socialist state to a liberal democracy were initiated by the Round Table talks which lasted from 6 February to 5 April 1989. Then, the long-awaited political changes were finally drafted. In constitutional terms, the 1952 Constitution of the People's Republic of Poland was amended first in April (the President and Senate were reinstated, political pluralism was introduced) and later in December 1989. The December Novelization introduced the rule of law into the system and renamed the country the RP. That was the time the Third RP came into existence in the eyes of the public. On the other hand, all the potential of the transformed state was not sufficiently prepared to adopt a new constitution. It was not until after the free parliamentary elections in 1991 that a political aura developed, conducive to carrying out the constitutional work. It was decided to implement the Small Constitution of 1992 first, due to intensive need to change the constitutional framework of the state. This act governed the relations between the legislative and executive authorities and the issue of local self-government. In this respect, the relevant provisions of the Constitution of the People's Republic of Poland were repealed and other matters, such as human and civil rights and freedoms, remained in force.

15. The text of the currently binding Constitution was drafted and adopted by the National Assembly (joined chambers of Parliament). The Constitution of 2 April 1997 was adopted by the Nation in constitutional referendum, and it marked the end of political transformation in Poland.

§2. CHARACTERISTICS OF THE POLISH STATE

I. Constitutionalism

16. Constitutionalism is a concept, which indicates many different points of reference and, consequently, the meaning of this term in Polish law and legal practice. In a broader perspective, it is a set of principles of the political system of the State which creates a model of exercising power limited by law, in particular by the Constitution as the act of the highest legal validity. In this meaning, constitutionalism creates the system of guarantees and instruments allowing citizens to be protected against arbitrary and unjustified action by the state authorities. This system is regulated by the laws serving as tools for mutual limitation of the exercise of power by its subjects. It is also the principle through which the values fundamental for the community, such as freedom of the press, association or equality, are protected and respected in the State. Thus, constitutionalism to a large extent exhausts the significance of such constitutional principles as (among others): the principle of a democratic form of government, the rule of law, separation of powers, civic society and political pluralism.

17. This norm is closely related in Polish science of the law and legal practice primarily to the principle of legality, expressed in Article 7 of the Constitution, according to which public authorities *act under and within the limits of the law.*

18. In a narrower sense, constitutionalism means that the Constitution is the highest law regulating fundamental issues, guaranteeing the standard of their implementation. The Constitution provides the basis for the exercise of power in the State and is directly applicable, binding equally all the entities in power.

19. The more concise meaning of this principle is expressed in Article 8 of the Polish Constitution, according to which the Constitution shall be the supreme law of the RP. The provisions of the Constitution are directly applicable, unless the Constitution provides otherwise.

20. When the Constitution was adopted in 1997, its supremacy was not subject to much controversy, whereas doubts and disputes occurred especially in the context of the paradigm of the positivist model of the judicial application of law and a judge being bound with the statutory law. Eventually, the principle was adopted, and the dispute over the courts' direct application of the Constitution was left to legal practitioners. Such disputes concerning the importance of this principle were raised particularly in the period of 1996–2008 between the Supreme Court (SC) and the SAC and the CT. Pursuant to the position taken in the SC's rulings (including the decisions: of 14 May 1996, III ARN 93/95; of 7 April 1998 I PKN 90/98; of 20 June 2000 I KZP 14/00) and the SAC (including the decision of 24 October 2000, V SA 613/00), the direct application of the constitutional provisions leads, in practice, to the situation where the court – recognising the inconsistency of the statutory provision of a lower rank with certain constitutional norm – may refuse to apply the provisions of the act.

21. However, pursuant to the position consistently developed in the jurisprudence of the CT (e.g., decisions: of 8 December 1999, SK 19/99; of 10 October 2000, P 8/99; of 24 June 1998, U 4/97; of 22 March 2000, P 12/98; of 31 January 2001, P 4/99; of 4 December 2001, SK 18/00), judges have no right to refuse to apply the provisions of a statute they consider to be unconstitutional, as only the CT is competent to perform the assessment and determination of the constitutionality of statutory norms.

22. This position was finally accepted in judicial decisions in the following years; both common and administrative courts acknowledged that allowing direct application of the Constitution by courts through refusal to apply the provisions of a statute declared unconstitutional in court judgments would lead to the situation of legal uncertainty and dualism of control over the constitutionality of statutory provisions (*inter alia*: SC judgments of 18 September 2002, III CKN 326/01, of 3 December 2008, V CSK 310/08; of 27 January 2010, II CSK 370/09; SAC judgments of 27 March 2008, I FSK 442/07; of 10 October 2017, II GSK 1954/16).

23. However, the supremacy of the Constitution imposes an obligation on the courts to refer a question of law to the CT whenever they consider the unconstitutional nature of the statutory regulation to be applied (Article 193 of the 1997 Constitution: *Any court may refer a question of law to the Constitutional Tribunal as to the conformity of a normative act to the Constitution, ratified international agreements or statute, if the answer to such question of law will determine an issue currently before such court*). The Tribunal's reply confirming the unconstitutional nature of the provision in question constitutes a legally admissible refusal to apply the provision in a particular case, while having universal effect, i.e., the loss of validity of such provision.

24. The concept of the 'pro-constitutional method of legal interpretation', as a particular kind of systemic interpretation, has been formulated based on the principle of the supremacy of the Constitution. Under this approach, in a situation when a specific provision allows for several possibilities of interpretation, the court is obliged to adopt the interpretation that meets constitutional norms, principles and values in the best manner (CT's decision of 15 May 2007, P 13/06, ruling of the SAC of 13 November 2013, II OPS 2/12). The supremacy of the Constitution means that a pro-constitutional interpretation should take precedence over a functional, purposeful, as well as internal systemic one, requiring the courts to follow such interpretation.

25. However, the case law specifies two situations in which the court may refuse to apply the provisions of a legal act; this happens when the content of the provision is 'clearly (content-related) inconsistent with the constitutional provision' and when 'a similar legal status was previously deemed by the Constitutional Tribunal as unconstitutional' (SAC judgment of 30 January 2018, II GSK 2706/17, SAC resolution of 16 October 2006, I FPS 2/06, SC judgment of 17 March 2016, V CSK 377/15 and 413/15). It should be noted that the refusal to apply the provision of a legal act with reference to the direct and supreme power of a constitutional norm in a court ruling has a different effect than a ruling on unconstitutionality issued by the CT. The former refers only to the parties to the proceedings and the case being considered (the *inter partes* effect), while the decision of the Tribunal on unconstitutionality is universally binding (the *erga omnes* effect).

26. In the last five years (2015–2020), the dispute over this aspect and the consequences of the direct applicability of constitutional norms and their supreme legal force were revived in judicial practice – a view has emerged in the study of constitutional law promoting the possibility for the adjudicating court to refuse the application of a law, without the need to refer to the CT; a political conflict surrounding the CT with its noticeable paralysis and loss of the ability to make impartial, apolitical rulings on the unconstitutionality of laws in the Constitution provided the basis for such an interpretation. This view – although expressed in statements of a journalistic and academic nature – has not yet been clearly confirmed in the jurisprudence of both common and administrative courts.

II. The Rule of Law

27. The rule of law (verbatim: the principle of a democratic state ruled by law) was introduced into Polish constitutional order during the first period of transition, on 29 December 1989, by way of an amendment to the Constitution of 1952. Its inspiration should be traced back to the German concept of the *Rechtsstaat* rather than the French *Etat de Droit* or Anglo-Saxon *Rule of Law*. Undoubtedly, the intention of the authors – namely the new parliament created for the first time as a result of partially free elections of June 1989 – was to separate clearly from the socialist rule of law, under which the State is actually not bound by any law, and where those in power do not bear any responsibility nor have any formal authority. The rule of law was supposed to mean that there are certain general, specific, known and accepted rules according to which the subjects of power are subordinated. It was therefore intended to be the antithesis of authority that is free to act and not obliged to explain its motives. The basic objective and the essence of the transformation were equated with this very principle. In the course of the lengthy work on the adoption of the new Constitution of 2 April 1997, there was no in-depth debate on the meaning and content of the notion of the rule of law, and at the same time its introduction was non-contentious, and it was included in all versions presented to the Constitutional Committee, confirming its importance as the inviolable foundation of the Polish political system. Nevertheless, lack of a wider debate caused the transplantation of the German concept of the *Rechtsstaat* to be successful only in the layer of the legal system, with no roots in social sphere.

28. In the science of Polish law, the principle of the democratic rule of law has been defined as a set of several components:

(a) There is a system of legal norms autonomous from the State and its authorities.
(b) The law is enacted democratically, by a body representing the nation, and its basic form is a statute, namely an act of parliament passed by means of a special procedure, ensuring the expression and fulfilment of the will of the nation.
(c) The Constitution guarantees the coherence of the legal order with the values and principles it expresses.
(d) The public authority must act within the limits of and under the law.
(e) The State is equipped with a system of guarantees regarding the observance of the law.

29. During the first eight years after the introduction of the principle of the rule of law into the Polish constitutional order, there were no other clauses adequate for a democratic and liberal state, and thus there were no proper standards of constitutionality of laws. As a result, the rule of law became a universal formula for establishing the standard of law in Poland, as well as an attempt to answer the question of how state bodies should operate in general, also beyond aspects of compliance with procedures and substantive law. Considerable margin of interpretation while giving meaning to this principle, especially at a time of dynamic changes in the law during the political transformation, quickly made it an extremely important instrument of case law. Frequent use of the formula of the rule of law by the CT after 1989 justifies the statement that it has become the ‘rule of rules’, a specific source and basis for the whole concept of developing and applying law in new reality.[1] As it was stressed in Polish literature, the principle of the rule of law has acquired a

1. A similar role in Hungarian legal practice has been played by the principle of inherent human dignity, understood as a source of individual rights. The deficit of constitutional norms reflecting the regime actually in force in the Republic of Hungary has been remedied by the Constitutional Court through the application of this formula, as well as through further interpretations leading to system of coherent principles of a liberal and democratic state – what the President of the Court, Laszlo Solyom, called the ‘invisible constitution’. *See* K.L. Scheppele, *A Comparative View of the Chief Justice Role*, 154 U. Pa. L. Rev. 1777 (2005–2006).

substantial dimension, became a set of principles and rules concerning the lawmaking process, as well as its content. As early as in the first ruling issued after the introduction of the rule of law, i.e., in the decision of 8 May 1990 (K 1/90), the CT stated that the constitutional formula of the rule of law imposes an obligation on the legislator to make laws so that they do not violate the principle of justice or the principle of equality as fundamental constitutional rights of citizens. In subsequent judgments the Tribunal derived the principle of protection of acquired rights from the principle of the rule of law (K 7/90), followed by: the right to a fair trial (decision of 7 January 1999, K 8/91), the prohibition of biomedical experimentation on human foetuses (decision of 17 March 1993, W 16/92), the right to protect conceived life (decision of 28 May 1997, K 26/96) and the right to privacy (decision of 24 June 1997, K 21/96). The content of the principle of the democratic rule of law in the CT's view was in fact created derivatively by specific values, perceived as ones requiring protection.

30. The moment of entry into force of the Constitution of 1997, in which the catalogue of rights and freedoms and the system of protecting them was regulated in great detail, ended this stage of creating interpretation of the clause of the democratic rule of law, while the formal interpretation thereof remained valid.

31. The formal dimension of the rule of law, shaped in the years 1989–1997, should be referred to as a set of principles and rules concerning the process of lawmaking and its validity. The set of such principles was defined in the Tribunal's jurisprudence as 'the principle of decent/reliable legislation'. These principles derive from the principle of protecting citizens' trust in the State, developed in the jurisprudence of the administrative judiciary and the CT. It requires the State to be loyal and honest towards the addressees of the standards it lays down (CT decision of 15 February 2005, K 48/04). Also, making and applying the law must be transparent and clear to citizens, and it cannot be any sort of a trap (*inter alia*, CT rulings of 15 July 1996, K 5/96; of 3 December 1996, K 25/95; of 25 November 1997, K 26/97; of 10 April 2001, U 7/00; of 5 November 2002, P 7/01; of 7 June 2004, P 4/03; of 15 February 2005, K 48/04; of 29 November 2006, SK 51/06; of 3 June 2008, K 42/07). In turn, the principle of citizen's trust in the State and the law imply that the addressee of the law (an individual) should be able to foresee the consequences of particular behaviour and events based on the applicable law and to expect the legislator not to change the rules in an arbitrary manner. The legal safety of an individual, connected to the certainty of the law, thus enables the predictability of the actions of state bodies.

32. The principle of citizens' trust in the State constitutes a source of more detailed rules, worked out in the jurisprudence of the CT, among which one should distinguish:

- The principle of the clarity of the provisions, according to which the law must be precise and clear, i.e., it must be formulated in such a way as to enable the addressee to determine the consequences of his/her conduct without difficulty (CT decision of 22 May 2002, K 6/02). The ambiguity of a provision may justify

finding it unconstitutional provided that it is so far-reaching that doubts or discrepancies resulting from its interpretation in judicial decisions cannot be removed (CT decision of 3 December 2002, P 13/02). This principle is also violated if an act contains concepts that are contradictory or allow for free interpretation (CT decision of 14 September 2001, SK 11/00).
– The prohibition of retroactivity. This prohibition is not uniform; the strictest requirements concern the provisions of criminal law and tax law, whereas others are not affected as much. However, the new legal provisions must not retroactively worsen the situation of an individual in any legal situation or area of law (CT decision of 25 September 2000, K 26/99).
– The order to comply with *vacatio legis*, i.e., the legislator's obligation to observe an adjustment period when implementing the law. The adjustment period is not set a priori, although Article 4 of the Act of 20 July 2000 on the promulgation of normative acts and certain other legal acts provides that in normal circumstances this period should last fourteen days. However, it must be set as appropriate depending on the subject matter and content of the newly enacted norms (CT decision of 20 December 1999, K 4/99). In view of some regulations, the Tribunal's jurisprudence has assumed that it should be much longer, e.g., changes in tax law should be communicated to taxpayers at least one month before the end of the previous tax year (decisions of the CT of 28 December 1995, K 28/95 and of 27 February 2002, K 47/01).
– The principle of protection of rights acquired legitimately, i.e., the prohibition of arbitrary abolition or limitation of subjective rights vested in an individual (including a legal person) and acquired in accordance with the law in force. This prohibition is not absolute; under this principle, however, the legislator is obliged to formulate the provisions (including interim ones) in such a way so as to provide the addressee of the standards with conditions to adapt to the new legal situation (decisions of the CT of 25 June 2002, K 45/01 and of 18 September 2006, SK 15/05). However, the Tribunal's jurisprudence has repeatedly seen a number of deviations from this principle on the grounds of the necessity to protect the economic interests of the State; this allowed, *inter alia*, for the limitation of the right to make pension adjustments (CT decisions of 22 October 2001, SK 16/01), veterans' rights (CT decision of 9 March 2004, K 12/02) or the abolition of tax benefits (CT judgment of 12 January 1995, K 12/94).

33. In conclusion, it should be added that numerous acts of the Polish public authorities, in particular of the central government, including legislative acts, have been challenged and disputed as violating the rule of law over the last five years. The protests in the years 2015–2017 originated mainly from the parliamentary and non-parliamentary opposition circles and NGOs (a.o. Polish Bar Council, Amnesty International Poland, Helsinki Foundation for Human Rights) that were against these decisions. Objections also take the form of statements issued by judicial bodies and courts (*see* further Part II., Chapter 5., §1., II., A. The Independence of the Judiciary) and the decisive actions of European Union (EU) bodies, including the Court of Justice of the European Union (CJEU), the Council of Europe and the United Nations (UN).

III. Principle of Legality

34. The Polish Constitution introduces the principle of legality independent of the rule of law. It is expressed in Article 7 of the Constitution of 1997, which states that '*The organs of public authority shall function on the basis of, and within the limits of, the law.*' Prior to the enactment of the Constitution, this principle was interpreted under the rule of law and was an essential part of it in its formal aspect; but during the course of constitutional work, it was decided to make it separate and to express it directly, in its own constitutional norm. The content of Article 7 refers to all public authorities – not only the legislature, the executive and the judiciary but also local self-government (which was emphasised by the CT in its decision of 29 October 2009, K 32/08) and all other institutions and bodies that perform the functions entrusted to such public authorities.

35. The principle of legality set out in Article 7 of the Constitution introduces a significant dichotomy between the status of an individual and a public authority; although the authority is obliged to demonstrate legal basis for each of its activities, each subject of the law (a person, as well as legal persons and entities without legal personality) may – pursuant to Article 31(1) of the Constitution – freely and in accordance with its own will shape its behaviour, and other entities are constitutionally prohibited from interfering with this sphere. No one shall be compelled to do that which is not required by law (Article 31(2) of the Constitution).

36. The principle of legality includes an injunction addressed to public authorities to act on the basis and within the scope of the law. All actions taken by public authorities must be based on an explicit competency vested in them. The scope of a public authority's operation, the course of proceedings, as well as the type of decision or action taken, must result from the provisions of generally applicable law. The sources of universally binding law are explicitly mentioned in the Polish Constitution – their catalogue is closed and their system is hierarchically structured (*see* Part I. Sources of Law). Consequently, the principle of legality means that any interference on the part of public authority into the legal sphere of an individual must be supported by specific provision of universally binding law, and all competencies of public authorities must be clearly and precisely defined in the provisions of universally binding law; they cannot be presumed (CT decision of 14 June 2006, K 53/05). According to the Tribunal the constitutional principle of legality dictates that bodies of authority may not act without a legal basis nor avoid the exercise of powers if binding legal norms impose certain obligations. The principle of legality is supplemented in this context with the essential guarantee, resulting from Article 77, paragraphs 1 and 2 of the Constitution, according to which: (1) everyone is entitled to compensation for loss caused by the unlawful conduct of public authority, and (2) no one shall be prevented from seeking redress for violations of freedoms or rights.

37. The principle of legality is also embedded in the statutory provisions in relation to public administration bodies – in accordance with Article 6 of the Code of Administrative Procedure, public administration bodies act on the basis of legal provisions.

IV. Separation of Powers

38. The principle of separation of powers has a long and turbulent history as far as Polish Constitutional Law is concerned. The first Polish Constitution, passed in 1791 (The Constitution of 3 May 1791), explicitly introduced in its Article 5 this principle as the basis of the constitutional monarchy, establishing the legislative, executive and judicial power. After regaining independence in 1918, the principle of separation of powers became the basis of the political system under the 1921 Constitution, while the next Constitution (1935) declared the departure from it, introducing concentration of power in the hands of the President as a principle (Article 2). The principle of unity of power in the State, i.e., rejection of the principle of separation of powers, was introduced by the Constitution of the People's Republic of Poland of 1952. The return to the separation of powers as the basic principle of the political system took place after full state sovereignty had been regained; more specifically, in 1992 the Small Constitution regulated the separation of the legislative power exercised by the Sejm and the Senate, the executive power exercised by the President and the Council of Ministers and the judiciary power, and entrusted it to the courts and tribunals. Between 1989 and 1992, the separation of powers was interpreted in accordance with the principle of the democratic rule of law.

39. The Constitution of 1997 introduces the principle of separation of powers in Article 10(1). The system of government of the RP shall be based on the separation of and balance between the legislative, executive and judicial powers. According to Article 10 section 2 Legislative power shall be vested in the Sejm and the Senate, executive power shall be vested in the President of the RP and the Council of Ministers, and the judicial power shall be vested in courts and tribunals. The authority is therefore divided into three functions, which the entities are assigned to. It is noteworthy that the President has been directly classified as the executive power, which raised considerable doubts as to his position and relations with other bodies of state power during the course of constitutional works and on some other occasions. According to Article 126 of the Constitution, which defines the political standing of this body, the President of the RP shall be the supreme representative of the RP and the guarantor of the continuity of state authority and shall ensure observance of the Constitution, safeguard the sovereignty and security of the State as well as the inviolability and integrity of its territory. These functions of the Head of State and the catalogue of competencies of the President (*see* Part II., Chapter 3., §3. Powers) as well as the lack of participation in the exercise of the current executive power indicate that his position among the entities of the executive power is difficult to consider as consistent with the wording of the Constitution and in the legal practice pertaining to the political system.

40. According to the CT's jurisprudence, the principle of separation of powers assumes that the system of state bodies should include internal mechanisms to prevent concentration and abuse of state power, at the same time guaranteeing respect for individual freedoms and rights. Each of the authorities should therefore have instruments at their disposal that enable them to deter the actions of others according to the checks and balance formula (CT judgment of 18 February 2004, P 21/02). Such instruments that would allow the executive to hinder the legislative authority include: the President's right of veto over laws passed by Parliament, the Government's exclusive legislative initiative regarding the budget law, or (although very limited in Polish constitutional regulations) the President's capacity to shorten the term of Parliament. In turn, the following can be pointed out as instruments of limiting the scope of executive authority by Parliament: instigating constitutional accountability of the President and ministers, granting the vote of confidence and the vote of no confidence over the Government, as well as control over the execution of the state budget by the Government.

41. As underlined by the Polish CT, the principle of separation of powers means that each of the three bodies should retain a minimum of essential competencies (decision of 29 November 2005, P 16/04). Thus, the exercise of the Sejm's control powers cannot lead to a violation of the powers of the Council of Ministers to manage government administration (CT decision of 14 April 1999, K 8/99).

42. The case law of the CT has so far established the view that the principle of separation of powers presupposes a specific way of defining the relationship between the judicial authority and the other authorities. Different forms of interaction and cooperation are possible in relations between the legislature and the executive, including the existence of an area in which the powers of the two authorities intersect or overlap. In contrast, relations between the judicial and other authorities must be based on the strict separation (CT judgment of 21 November 1994, K 6/94). The principle of separation of powers is therefore complemented by the autonomy of courts and the independence of judges, as set out in Article 178 of the Constitution. The strict separation of the judiciary is manifested in its specific competency to administer the justice, but its relations with other authorities are preserved. The basis of the courts' activity is constituted by laws, i.e., acts of parliament, judges are appointed by the President of the RP, and the Minister of Justice exercises administrative supervision of common courts (*inter alia*: CT judgment of 19 July 2005, K 28/04).

43. However, recent years have brought serious controversies regarding the way in which judicial authority is formed and the scope of administrative supervision over it. In 2015, the President refused to take an oath from constitutional judges, elected by the previous parliament as being elected against the principle of tenure, while the newly elected parliament passed an amendment to the Law on the CT in November, and the second one, in December 2015, invalidated the previous choice and elected five new judges to replace those already elected. A law was also passed to change the structure and mode of working of the Polish CT, which was immediately declared unconstitutional by the Tribunal itself in March 2016. Eventually, new laws on the CT were passed in late 2016.

44. In 2017, the Parliament passed an act amending the Law on the System of Common Courts, introducing more extensive administrative supervision of the Minister of Justice over courts than had been the case so far. In addition, a new law on the National Council of the Judiciary (NCJ) (a constitutional body guarding the independence of courts) was adopted, as well as the amendment to the Law on the SC, which provided for the retirement of several judges, with the Minister of Justice being empowered to decide on their further stay. It was vetoed by the President and the new Law on the SC was adopted upon his initiative in 2017. This in turn created two new SC chambers in 2018: the Disciplinary Chamber and the Extraordinary Control and Public Affairs Chamber. Yet, the most controversial issue from the point of view of the independence of the judiciary has been the mode of appointment of new judges, including SC judges by the NCJ, which, under the new law, has been formed solely by the Parliament. A provision of the Polish Constitution stipulates that this same body, which upholds judicial independence and judicial independence, shall be composed of: the First President of the SC, the Minister of Justice, the President of the SAC and an individual appointed by the President of the Republic and fifteen judges selected from among the judges of the SC, common courts, administrative courts and military courts; also four members chosen by the Sejm from among its Deputies and two members chosen by the Senate from among its Senators (Article 187).

45. Until the new NCJ law was passed, judges had been appointed to it by the relevant judicial bodies, whereas the new law introduced the election of judges to the NCJ by the Sejm, which stands in clear contradiction to the interpretation of this provision of the Constitution accepted to date. However, in March 2019, the CT concluded that the provisions on appointing members of the new NCJ from among judges by the Sejm were constitutionally valid. It also declared the provision allowing for an appeal to the SAC against NCJ resolutions on the selection of candidates for judges of the SC unconstitutional, thus making the NCJ decisions final.

46. At the turn of 2019–2020, controversy was further exacerbated by the enactment and implementation of amendments to the legislation on the judiciary, which increased the disciplinary accountability of judges and the potential for interference by other authorities. The implementation of these reforms has triggered a negative reaction from the opposition, legal and expert bodies in Poland and throughout Europe as well as from the EU and the courts themselves.

47. To illustrate this, the resolution of the three Chambers of the SC of 23 January 2019 (BSA I-4110-1/20), in which the SC accepted that if a person appointed as a judge at the request of the NCJ formed in accordance with the new regulations (i.e., in accordance with the procedure set out in the Act of 8 December 2017) is sitting in the composition of the SC, the court may be deemed unduly (contrary to the law) filled. The same applies when a judge appointed in such a manner adjudicates within the composition of a common court, 'if the defective appointment causes, under specific circumstances, a breach of the standards of independence within the meaning of Article 45(1) of the Constitution, Article 47 of the Charter of

Fundamental Rights of the European Union and Article 6(1) of the Convention for the Protection of Human Rights and Fundamental Freedoms'.

48. One important element of the separation of powers is the directive of cooperation, indicated in the Preamble to the Constitution. It requires the entities of the public authorities of the RP to respect each other's scope of tasks, competencies and the dignity of offices and their representatives, to express mutual loyalty, act in good faith, inform each other about initiatives, be prepared to cooperate and make arrangements, then observe and implement them diligently (decision of the CT of 20 May 2009, Kpt 2/08). The relation between the directive of cooperation and the principle of separation of powers is clear – on the one hand, there are mechanisms preventing the concentration of power functions and ensuring a relative balance of bodies involved. On the other hand, it cannot lead to their complete separation and autonomy of the decisions. The formula of cooperation applies to both individual segments of the separated power and the bodies operating in a given segment.

49. Apart from the general obligation to cooperate, the Constitution requires the President to act together with the Prime Minister and the relevant minister in matters of foreign policy. This is related to the division of powers between the executive bodies. This division is intended to prevent concentration of power. However, it cannot lead to paralysis of, e.g., foreign policy. Hence, the Constitution forces the obligation of the Head of State to cooperate when the President does one of the following as the State's representative in external relations: (1) ratification and denunciation of international agreements, of which the Sejm and the Senate shall be notified, (2) appointment and dismissal of the authorised representatives of the RP in other States and at international organisations, (3) accepts letters of authorisation and of dismissal of diplomatic representatives in other States and international organisations accredited to him.

50. The Constitution of the RP of 1997 provides for particularly precise directives on cooperation in the field of competencies and relations between the legislative and executive bodies in matters related to security. According to Article 89, ratification of an international agreement by the RP, as well as renunciation thereof, shall require prior consent granted by statute – if such agreement concerns, among other things, peace, alliances, political or military treaties. Such an action therefore requires the expression of will by the Parliament; this is also the case with respect to issues regulated by Article 117 of the Constitution, and therefore the principles for deployment of the Armed Forces beyond the borders of the RP and the principles for the presence of foreign troops on the territory of the RP and the principles for their movement within that territory. These matters are regulated by ratified international agreements and acts. However, the legislator is bound by the presidential functions of a guardian of the sovereignty and security of the State as well as the inviolability and integrity of its territory, as well as the Supreme Commander of the Armed Forces of the RP (Articles 126 and 134 of the Polish Constitution). It must also take into account the functions entrusted to the Council of Ministers: ensuring the internal and external security of the State and the general management of the country's defence (Article 146 of the Polish Constitution).

51. The cooperation also includes the competency of the Sejm to decide on the state of war. Pursuant to Article 116 of the Constitution, the Sejm may adopt a resolution on the state of war only in the event of armed aggression against the territory of the RP or when an obligation of common defence against aggression arises by virtue of international agreements. If the Sejm cannot assemble for a sitting, the President of the Republic may declare the state of war. Additionally, the institution of countersignature ensures the participation of the Prime Minister in this act. Concluding peace, on the other hand, is constitutionally reserved as the exclusive competency of the Sejm.

52. With regard to states of emergency, the Constitution of the RP also distributes powers between the Government and the Head of State, while introducing mechanisms of cooperation pertaining also to the Sejm. Martial law and state of emergency may be introduced by the President at the request of the Council of Ministers. The Sejm, on the other hand, approves regulations with the force of a law issued during martial-law period, decides on the extension of the state of emergency and state of natural disaster (announced by the Government), and also examines the regulation on the introduction of both martial law or state of emergency (*see* further Part V. Extraordinary Measures: Martial Law, a State of Emergency or a State of Natural Disaster).

V. National Sovereignty and Forms of Democracy

53. Pursuant to Article 4(1) of the Constitution, supreme power in the RP shall be vested in the Nation. According to the Preamble of the Polish Constitution, the Nation is understood as all citizens of the Republic. This phrase is unanimously recognised in the Polish legal science as separating the concept of political community from ethnic categories. The Preamble also refers to the historical and political conditions of the existence of the Nation and the enactment of the Constitution, as it begins with words: 'Having regard for the existence and future of our Homeland, having regained in 1989 the possibility of a sovereign and democratic determination of its fate, we, the Polish Nation – all citizens of the Republic of Poland.'

54. The power of the Nation is supreme. It is – as phrased in the Polish legal science – a primary and permanent power, i.e., invariable over time, indivisible and inalienable.

55. Equipping the Nation with supreme power as a political community in the wording of the Constitution relates to the principle of the republican form of government, already expressed in the name of the State – the 'Republic' derives from the Latin *res publica*, and although it originally meant a common good, i.e., simply the State, with time its meaning came closer to that of the republic. The principle of the sovereignty of the Nation should also be interpreted in connection with the principle formulated in Article 1 of the Constitution which articulates the common good.

This concept, rooted in the Polish history of constitutionalism since the Constitution of 1935, tends to be interpreted in the tradition of social teaching of the Catholic Church and neo-Thomism. Under this concept, the common good is a set of conditions that enable members of a community to achieve the goals they themselves consider proper or to pursue own rational values for the sake of which they can work together within the community.

56. Article 4(2) of the Constitution indicates two forms of the exercise of power by the Nation – through representatives and in person. Representative democracy is listed first and constitutes a principle, while forms of direct democracy are exceptional and complementary (CT decision of 20 July 2011, K 9/11).

57. Representative democracy means that power is exercised in the name of the Nation through representatives; therefore, the basic form of expression of will by the Nation is the regular general elections of representative bodies, provided they are universal, equal, direct and proportional and conducted by secret ballot (Articles 96 and 97 of the Constitution). The primary representative body is the Parliament, with both its chambers (the Sejm and the Senate) composed of Deputies and Senators who are considered to be the representatives of the Nation (Articles 104 and 108 of the Constitution). Consequently, Members of Parliament (MPs) have a free mandate, i.e., they are not bound by the instructions of their voters, nor can they be dismissed by them during their term of office – as soon as they obtain a mandate, they become representatives of the whole Nation, and not only of their voters or their constituency. The President of the RP is also elected by universal suffrage, but the Constitution does not define the Head of State as a representative of the Nation, but as the highest representative of the State.

58. Local self-government bodies are also of representative nature – both collegiate bodies, i.e., commune councils, district councils, the province (*Voivodeship*) local parliaments (*Sejmik*); and the executive bodies presidents, mayors and commune heads (the name of the body depends on the size and nature of the commune). These bodies, however, do not represent the Nation, but the local communities, i.e., the residents living on the territory covered by these local government units (communes, districts, voivodeships).

59. The democratic form of exercising power is closely related to the constitutional principle and guarantees of political pluralism expressed in Article 11 of the Constitution. According to it, the Republic shall ensure freedom for the creation and functioning of political parties that are founded on the principle of voluntariness and upon the equality of Polish citizens, and their purpose shall be to influence the formulation of the policy of the State by democratic means.

60. The financing of political parties is transparent. Furthermore, the Constitution guarantees the freedom for the creation and functioning of trade unions, organisations of farmers, as well as other societies, citizens' movements, voluntary associations and foundations (Article 12). However, under Article 13 of the Constitution, the existence of political parties and other organisations whose programmes are based upon totalitarian methods and the modes of activity of Nazism, fascism and communism, as well as those whose programmes or activities sanction racial or national hatred, the application of violence for the purpose of obtaining power or to influence the state policy, or provide for the secrecy of their own structure or membership, shall be prohibited. The CT has been entrusted with the possibility to review the constitutionality of the objectives and activities of political parties.

61. In addition, the Constitution contains substantial guarantees of democratic scrutiny over the exercise of power, in particular freedom of the press (Article 14) and the right of citizens to be informed about the activities of public authorities and persons discharging public functions (Article 61).

62. The other form of governance of the Nation is direct democracy. Polish Constitutional Law identifies several forms of expressing the Nation's will directly; the most important of them is a nationwide referendum, provided for in Article 125 of the Constitution, as an expression of will by citizens entitled to vote on 'matters of particular importance to the State' (*see* Part II., Chapter 1., §3. Referendum). It is binding, provided that more than half of those entitled to vote actively participate in it. The Constitution also provides for two specific modes of referendum: the first (confirmatory referendum) on the approval of an amendment to the Constitution in so far as it amends provisions relating to the principles of the system or to rights and freedoms or the amendment of the Constitution itself (Article 235(6)) and the other on the consent to the ratification of an international agreement delegating the powers of the authorities of the State in certain matters to an international organisation or body (Article 90(3)). In the chapter dedicated to local self-government, the Constitution also provides for this form of democracy at the local level (Article 170). The Constitution does not, however, stipulate any obligation to hold a referendum in every possible situation; it is always subject to the initiative or agreement of the representative body.

63. Another form of direct democracy, provided for in the Polish constitutional order, is the civic initiative. According to Article 118 of the Polish Constitution, a group of at least 100,000 citizens entitled to vote in general elections have the right to submit their bill to the Parliament. However, citizens cannot pass the law or repeal it in a referendum.

64. In practice, direct democracy procedures are used by citizens rather inefficiently. The final form of any decision being the subject of a referendum is chosen by the body that executes it (most often it is the Parliament that adopts the law in the course of regular legislative procedure).

VI. State Sovereignty

65. The principle of sovereignty of the Nation expressed in Article 4 of the Constitution is closely related to the principle of sovereignty of the State addressed by the Polish Constitution on several occasions. However, it was not established as a separate political principle in Chapter I of the Constitution. This principle is mentioned in Article 126(2) which points out that one of the President's tasks is to safeguard the sovereignty of the State, and the MPs also undertake to safeguard it in the wording of their oath (Article 104(2)).

66. The sovereignty of the State means the ability to decide on internal matters and to independently decide on international obligations. In this context, the provisions of the Constitution that determine the form and scope of integration processes are of particular significance. Current Polish Constitution was adopted in 1997, during Poland's efforts to join the EU. However, the constitutional provision had already been laid down for the delegation of powers of state authorities in certain matters to an international organisation or body. Article 90, placed in the sources of law chapter, stipulates that such a transfer shall take place by means of an international agreement ratified by the President after obtaining the consent of the Parliament or the Nation in a special mode, i.e., by means of a law passed by the Sejm by the two-thirds majority vote in the presence of at least half of the statutory number of Deputies, or by means of a nationwide referendum. The constitutional regulation does not determine the extent to which the powers of the state authorities may be delegated; it only indicates that powers may be delegated 'in certain matters'. The Polish Constitutionalists emphasise that integration processes do not mean the transfer of sovereignty, but only the transfer of competencies, i.e., the limitation of the exercise of sovereign power – and not the power itself. These competencies cannot be delegated universally, nor can they be delegated in respect of all matters in a given field. As the CT indicated, 'It is necessary to define precisely the fields and to indicate the scope of the competencies covered by the delegation' (CT judgment of 11 May 2005, K 18/04).

67. The issue of Poland's sovereignty is also linked to the so-called constitutional identity of the State. According to the Treaty on European Union (TEU) (Article 4(2)), the EU is obliged to respect the 'national identities' of Member States, 'inherent in their fundamental structures, political and constitutional'. In its 2007 judgment on the constitutionality of the Lisbon Treaty, the Polish CT defined constitutional identity as a notion designating the 'core' of the foundations of a state's system, a matter which is not subject to a delegation of competency in its field to international bodies or organisations under Article 90 of the Constitution. Among such matters covered by the total ban on delegation, the Tribunal included provisions defining the fundamental principles of the Constitution and provisions concerning the rights of the individual, in particular the requirement to ensure the protection of human dignity and constitutional rights, the principle of statehood, the principle of democracy, the principle of the rule of law, the principle of social justice, the principle of subsidiarity, as well as the requirement to ensure better implementation of constitutional values and the prohibition of delegation of legislative power and competency to create competencies (CT decision of 24 November 2010, K 32/09).

VII. Autonomy of Churches, Religious Impartiality of the State

68. The relationship between churches and the State and the position of religious associations in Poland are regulated by the provisions of Article 25, which bears the rank of a constitutional rule. These relations are based on three principles:

(1) equality of churches and religious associations;
(2) impartiality of public authorities in matters of religious, ideological and philosophical beliefs and freedom of expression, closely related to freedom of conscience and religion guaranteed by Article 53 of the Constitution;
(3) autonomy of churches and religious associations.

69. The principle of equality of churches and religious associations means that all churches and religious associations sharing a common essential characteristic shall be treated equally. At the same time, this principle assumes different treatment of churches and religious associations which do not have a common essential feature in terms of a given regulation (CT judgment of 2 April 2003, K 13/02). Such a distinguishing feature is primarily different regulation of the relations between them and the State – in accordance with Article 25(4, 5) of the Constitution, this regulation is consensual in nature, which means that an agreement concluded between the public authorities and the authorities of that church constitutes the basis of the statutory regulation concerning the status of that church. With regard to the Roman Catholic Church, the relations between the RP and the Catholic Church shall be determined by the international treaty (*Konkordat*) concluded with the Holy See and by statute. As for the other churches, their legal situation is governed by agreements concluded by the Council of Ministers with the authorities of the relevant church or religious association, and on the basis of such an agreement a law is passed to regulate their legal situation. The difference in treatment of the Catholic Church and the other churches is justified by the fact that only the Holy See is a subject of international law.

70. It is noteworthy that the discussed constitutional provision concerns an already existing situation – all laws regulating the situation of churches and religious associations date back to the period before the Constitution of 1997 entered into force – thus, no law regulating the relations between the State and religious associations has been issued under the procedure provided for in the Constitution so far.

71. As indicated by the case law of the CT and the legal scholars' comments, the Polish constitutional regulation clearly follows the system of separation of the

State and churches and religious associations, and it is not possible to grant the State a religious character, although at the same time Article 25(4) and the concordat reflect the dominant position of the Catholic Church in the religious structure of the RP (hence, among others, the CT judgment of 2 December 2009, U 10/07).

72. The principle of public authorities' impartiality in matters of religious, ideological and philosophical beliefs sets out the prohibition of state authorities' interference in the sphere of religion and ideology and the functioning of churches and relations between them (CT decision of 2 April 2003, K 13/02). It also means that public authorities are forbidden to take a stance on the truthfulness of the views expressed by the theology of particular faiths or by particular philosophical trends (CT decision of 14 February 2009, K 55/07). In the same ruling, however, the Tribunal stated that the principle of impartiality of public authorities in matters of religious, ideological and philosophical beliefs does not preclude the State's commitment to the exercise of freedom of conscience and religion and to enable citizens to satisfy their needs in the religious sphere, in particular the state funding of schools and universities run by religious communities.

73. The principle of mutual independence and autonomy of the State and of churches and religious associations shall mean the prohibition of interference by public authorities in the internal affairs of religious communities, as well as the prohibition of the influence of church authorities on decisions and actions of the state authority. However, the internal law of religious communities is recognised in practice – on similar terms as the law of a foreign State, i.e., as the law applicable to members of the community and its authorities – also in external relations. However, this does not mean that the subordination to state law can be excluded pursuant to the norms of the church law. The concept of the autonomy of churches and religious associations pertains to their internal sphere of operation – independent determination of their internal affairs, in particular, determination of the content of faith, and organisational structures: that is, representation and authorities.

§3. State Territory

74. Pursuant to Article 3 of the Constitution, Poland is a unitary state. This applies primarily to its territorial structure. Therefore, it is impossible to distinguish any autonomous regions in Poland with separate bodies and legislative powers. However, this does not mean that the territory of the State is free from territorial division.

75. As provided for in Article 15 of the Constitution, the territorial system of the RP shall ensure the decentralisation of public power. It is one of the basic principles of the political system. Its importance is emphasised by placing it in the first chapter of the Basic Law. The Constitution also indicates the rules which should be followed by the legislator when establishing the territorial structure of the country. First of all, the legislator should take into consideration social, economic or cultural ties and ensure that territorial units are able to perform public tasks.

76. The territorial division is related to the decentralisation of the tasks of the State. The tasks are delegated under the principle of dualism of structures to be performed by the Government and the local self-government administration bodies. Decentralisation applies primarily to the executive authority. Legislative and judicial authorities are not subject to decentralisation, although some legislative powers are provided for the benefit of territorial self-government administration bodies (mainly a voivode – a representative of the Council of Ministers in a voivodeship/province) and local self-government administration (at all levels – commune, district, voivodeship). In principle, they mean the possibility of executing acts in the form of local legal enactments included in Article 94 of the Constitution.

77. Territorial body of government administration is an extremely important element of civic society, as it allows citizens to organise themselves and make decisions on the most important issues concerning local communities. The importance of local government as an institution of civic society is underlined by the fact that it is treated as a self-governing community created by law by all inhabitants of the basic units of territorial division. On the other hand, the tasks and competencies of local government are to be carried out in accordance with the principle of subsidiarity, i.e., they should be fulfilled at the lowest possible level (commune), assuming that they are delegated to higher levels (district or voivodeship) when the volume of the tasks exceeds the organisational capacity of a lower level unit.

§4. Population and Demographics

78. The RP is a fairly large country located in Central Europe. It stretches between the Baltic Sea in the north and the Sudeten and Carpathian Mountains in the south, predominantly in the basins of the Vistula and Oder. The area of the country is 312,679 sq. km. To the north, Poland borders Russia (with its Kaliningrad Oblast) and Lithuania, Belarus and Ukraine to the east, Slovakia and the Czech Republic to the south, and Germany to the west. Most of Poland's northern border is the Baltic Sea coast.

79. Poland is a unitary state divided into sixteen voivodeships: mazowieckie, śląskie, wielkopolskie, małopolskie, dolnośląskie, łódzkie, pomorskie, lubelskie, podkarpackie, kujawsko-pomorskie, zachodniopomorskie, warmińsko-mazurskie, świętokrzyskie, podlaskie, lubuskie and opolskie. Neither overseas territories nor autonomous areas constitute a part of the territory of Poland.

80. Poland is inhabited by 38,383 thousand people (as of December 2019). The population is rather ethnically uniform. Polish nationality in the National Census of Population and Housing in 2011 was declared by 97% of the population. The remaining 3% of the population are representatives of nine national minorities (Belarusians, Czechs, Lithuanians, Germans, Armenians, Russians, Slovaks, Ukrainians and Jews) and four ethnic minorities (Karaims, Lemkos, Roma and Tartars). Moreover, the region of pomorskie voivodeship is inhabited by Kashubians, who also speak their own dialect. The largest national minority in Poland is represented by Germans.

Part I. Sources of Law

Chapter 1. Characteristics of the Constitutional System of Sources of Law

§1. Statutory Law System

81. A positivist concept of law has been adopted in the Polish Constitution. Consequently, the law constitutes a set of norms of conduct, secured by sanctions by the State and coming from public authority, i.e., from bodies equipped with the power to legislate (e.g., statute) or to recognise (e.g., an international agreement) such norms.

82. The legal norms described in this manner must also be associated with values stemming from the law of nature (e.g., the inherent and inalienable dignity of the human being). These values are treated as a benchmark for positive solutions. It is generally accepted that the sources of law in Poland do not include: custom and customary law, constitutional conventions and dissonance, court rulings, including those issued by international courts, as well as statements of legal doctrine and the science of law. Instead, they constitute important interpretative guidelines for the legal norms present in the sources of law. Although court rulings are not classified as sources of law, they are binding according to the rules provided for in the relevant court procedures (criminal, civil, administrative). In principle, court rulings bind entities *inter partes*, whereas CT rulings are effective *erga omnes*. Rulings of international courts remain valid pursuant to the rules provided for in international law (according to Article 9 of the Constitution, the RP shall respect international law binding upon it).

83. Therefore, the basic assumption of the sources of law system in Poland is that normative acts originating from the authorities specified and described in the Constitution are treated as sources of law and issued in compliance with lawmaking competency. First of all, it concerns the Constitution, statutes and regulations. Moreover, these will be such acts which contain new legal norms, i.e., orders or prohibitions of certain repetitive behaviour. Under the rule of the Constitution of 2 April 1997, the basic criteria for inclusion into normative acts were indicated by the CT in its judgments of 12 July 2001, SK 1/01 and 22 September 2006, U 4/06.

84. This original arrangement (constitution-legislation-regulation) is modified by the category of multicentricity of the system, for which Article 9 of the Constitution is of fundamental importance. This category includes both international law (in addition to international agreements, also unilateral acts, general principles, custom and precedents) and supranational law (EU law, established by bodies of a supranational organisation). Multicentricity assumes the functioning of many law-making centres, which create systems of sources of law based on different rules. These systems co-exist and are to be interpreted in mutually supportive way (CT decision of 11 May 2005, K 18/04 on the constitutionality of the Accession Treaty).

§2. Dichotomy: Universally and Internally Binding Sources of Law

85. Another assumption of the sources of law system is their dichotomous split into subsystems of the universally binding law and of the internally applicable acts. Both these categories are classified as sources of law.

86. According to the view expressed in CT judgment of 28 June 2000, K 25/99, only the universally binding law may serve as a legal foundation for decisions issued to citizens, legal persons and other entities. It may shape the legal situations of entities, i.e., set out obligations, grant powers and authorisations.

87. The Constitution clearly defines the categories of acts for which we should presume their normativity and universal validity. These are the acts indicated in Articles 87 (Constitution, statutes, ratified international agreements, regulations, local law acts) and 234 (regulations having the force of statute). No such presumption is made in relation to other categories interpreted from the Constitution, such as the rules of the Sejm and the Senate or collective labour agreements and others. This means that their normative and universally binding character should be proved *in concreto*. The Constitution does not grant these acts the indicated attribute directly, but only allows for such qualification.

88. Acts of internal law are described in Article 93 of the Polish Constitution (*see* Part I., Chapter 8. Sources of Internal Law: Characteristics). They may contain norms addressed to subordinate entities within an organisational structure, such as a ministry or an office.

§3. Hierarchy of Universally Binding Sources of Law

89. The underlying constructional assumption of the sources of law system is its hierarchical structure. In accordance with Article 8(1), the Polish Constitution is the supreme law of the RP. Therefore, it has the highest legal validity in the system, and as a consequence, it also has a derogatory power – namely, an act of law considered to be unconstitutional loses its validity. The lower level is the level of statutory regulations, which concretise the provisions of the Constitution. The consequence of this relation is a requirement to provide details of constitutional regulations and a ban on issuing norms that would be unconstitutional. A lower legal validity is assigned to executive regulations.

§4. Official Publication

90. Polish doctrine expresses certain general postulates concerning the promulgation of normative acts. It is treated as a core element of legal culture (according to the principle *leges instituuntur cum promulgantur*). Promulgation is a *sine qua non* for the rule's legally binding character. It is not a matter of making normative acts public in general, but of their official publication. The effects of such promulgation are therefore produced solely by the announcement of normative acts in the official publication designated for that purpose.

91. According to Article 88, the condition precedent for the coming into force of statutes, regulations and enactments of local law shall be the promulgation thereof. International agreements ratified with prior consent granted by statute shall be promulgated in accordance with the procedures required for statutes.

92. The obligation of promulgation relates to acts universally binding or internal ones. Normative acts are in principle promulgated in the form of an electronic document.

93. Universally binding sources of law shall be published in the Journal of Laws of the RP and shall enter into force – in general – fourteen days after being promulgated. A given act may stipulate a longer period of so-called *vacatio legis*. In justified cases, normative acts may come into force within a period shorter than fourteen days. Exceptionally, when an important interest of the State requires the immediate entry into force of a normative act, the act can enter into force on the date of promulgation.

94. In order to promulgate normative acts and certain other legal acts, the following official journals are issued: the Journal of Laws of the RP, the Official Gazette of the RP *Monitor Polski*, the official journals of ministers in charge of government administration departments, the official journals of central offices and voivodeship official journals.

Chapter 2. The Constitution

§1. Characteristics

95. The Constitution is being credited as the most prominent source of universally binding law and the entire state system derives its legitimacy from it. In the formal and legal sense, therefore, the Constitution is a normative act comprehensively regulating the political system of the State. In the sociological sense, the Constitution is treated as a social contract, in which the most important values forming national identity are contained. The constitutional identity is developed by treating the formal, legal and sociological phenomenon together.

96. Traditionally, the Constitution is characterised by three specific features that distinguish it from other statutes. First of all, the special form which highlights the specific name of this (the Constitution) and special mode of its enactment (the Constitution of the RP of 1997 was enacted by the Nation in a referendum, the text was prepared by the National Assembly) and passing amendments (prescribed by Article 235 of the Constitution). Second, the Constitution's content is very specific; on the one hand, it concerns the whole system of the State, on the other hand, it regulates only the basic issues referring to individual laws for details. The third special feature is its legal validity. According to Article 8 of the Constitution, it is the supreme law of the RP. This feature gives rise to the repeal of unconstitutional acts by constitutional review.

97. In the context of relations with the European law, in its judgment concerning the Treaty of Accession (CT decision of 11 May 2005, K 18/04) the CT stressed that the Constitution remains 'the supreme law of the Republic of Poland' in relation to all international agreements binding the RP. It also relates to ratified international agreements on the delegation of competency 'in certain matters'. On the territory of the RP, the Constitution enjoys priority of validity and application. The aforesaid position was also confirmed in the judgment concerning the Treaty of Lisbon (judgment of the CT of 24 November 2010, K 32/09). However, as was mentioned above, the Constitution also contains Article 9, according to which the RP shall respect international laws binding upon it. The relationship between these legal systems is therefore not hierarchical, but multicentric.

98. The Constitution is directly applicable, unless the Constitution itself provides otherwise (Article 8(2)) of the Polish Constitution). In other words, the act in its provisions contains specific, defined, precise and unambiguous (self-executing) norms. They do not need the so-called intermediary act to be applied and may constitute the basis for actions, decisions or norms. A special kind of direct application of the constitutional norms is exercised by courts (*see* more: General Introduction, §2. Constitutionalism). The provisions of the Constitution are considered as the legal basis also for judicial decisions.

99. Polish doctrine finds the 'constitutional act' different from the Constitution. Such an act is equal in legal force to the Constitution. There is currently only one type of constitutional act in Poland – A bill to amend the Constitution (Article 235), which can be passed in special procedure (*see* Chapter 2., §2. Amending the Constitution). It has no autonomous normative content; it amends or supplements the Constitution. After its entry into force, the provisions of the amending act are incorporated into the Constitution.

§2. Amending the Constitution

100. According to Article 235 of the Constitution of 1997, a bill to amend it may be submitted by: at least one-fifth of the statutory number of Deputies, the Senate or the President of the Republic. Amendments require a statute adopted by the Sejm by the majority of at least two-thirds of votes in the presence of at least half of the statutory number of Deputies. The amending statute shall be adopted in the same wording by the Senate by the absolute majority of votes in the presence of at least half of the statutory number of Senators. Within this procedure, the Senate acts as a veto player.

101. In case of the amendment procedure, the Constitution requires a confirmatory referendum. If a bill relates to the provisions of Chapters I, II or XII of the Constitution, at least one-fifth of the statutory number of Deputies, the Senate or the President may require holding of such a referendum. The amendment to the Constitution shall be accepted if the majority of those voting express support for it. However, the requirement of the referendum in scope of Chapters I, II and XII does not equal an eternity clause.

102. Only Article 30, guaranteeing human dignity, can be considered as the only unamendable provision. According to the Constitution, the dignity of the person shall be inviolable. The respect and protection thereof shall be the obligation of public authorities. Such authority is upon either the legislative power (the Sejm and the Senate) or the CT assessing legislation. Nevertheless, the Constitution does not provide *expressis verbis* regulations in terms of unamendability.

103. Additionally, the competency of the CT to assess the constitutional amendment remains uncertain. As stated in Article 188, the Tribunal shall adjudicate the conformity of statutes to the Constitution. Only if we assume that a 'statute' also means a 'statute to amend the Constitution', we can correlate the competency of the Tribunal to the above-mentioned procedure. However, the adjudication process could relate only to the required procedure and competencies of the Sejm and the Senate acting as the amending power.

104. The Constitution of 1997 has been formally amended two times with no legal or political reservations. The first amendment occurred in relation to the European Arrest Warrant (EAW) in 2006. The second was connected to the right to be elected to the Sejm or the Senate; since 2009 person who was sentenced to imprisonment by a final judgment for an intentional indictable offence cannot be elected.

Chapter 3. Treaties

§1. The Treaty-Making Power

105. The Polish Constitution regulates the following matters separately: conclusion of international agreements, ratification and granting consent to the ratification of treaties. These competencies have been assigned to different bodies within the executive and legislative power, with the incidental participation of the Nation expressing its views through a referendum.

106. According to the Constitution, the Council of Ministers has the competency to conclude international agreements requiring ratification. The Council of Ministers also approves and denounces other international agreements that do not require ratification. This stems from the position of this body, whose constitutional task is to conduct the foreign policy of the RP.

107. Ratification is the legal form of the RP being bound by international agreements and certain specific legal acts of the EU. Since the President of the RP is the highest representative of the State in external relations, this office has been given exclusive competency to ratify and denounce international agreements. The Constitution provides for three procedures for the ratification. Two of them require consent given in statute (Article 89(1) and Article 90 of the Constitution). The third procedure, concerning international agreements that do not require the consent for ratification in statute, is limited to imposing an obligation on the Prime Minister to notify the Sejm of any intention to submit an agreement for ratification to the President (Article 89(2) of the Constitution).

108. The competency to grant consent to ratify certain international agreements or to denounce them has been vested in the Parliament. According to Article 89(1), ratification of an international agreement by the RP, as well as denunciation thereof, shall require prior consent granted by statute – if such agreement concerns: (1) peace, alliances, political or military treaties; (2) freedoms, rights or obligations of citizens, as specified in the Constitution; (3) the RP's membership in an international organisation; (4) considerable financial responsibilities imposed on the State; (5) matters regulated by statute or those in respect of which the Constitution requires the form of statute. In the absence of specific regulations concerning the procedure for the enactment of a law expressing consent to ratification, the requirements of the ordinary legislative procedure shall apply. This means that the Sejm passes a bill by simple majority of votes in the presence of at least half of the statutory number of Deputies.

109. A separate procedure is provided for in relation to integration agreements. Article 90 of the Constitution, incorporated into the Constitution with the intention of regulating the procedure for accession to the EU, referred to as the 'integration clause', introduces a specific procedure for the ratification of international agreements under which Poland intends to 'delegate the competency of organs of State authority in relation to certain matters to an international organization or international institution'.

110. According to Article 90 of the Constitution, a statute expressing consent to ratify an international agreement, for example, shall be passed by the Sejm by the two-thirds majority vote in the presence of at least half of the statutory number of Deputies, and by the Senate by the two-thirds majority vote in the presence of at least half of the statutory number of Senators. Alternatively, the consent may be granted by a nationwide referendum. Any resolution in respect of the choice of procedure for granting consent to ratification shall be taken by the Sejm by the absolute majority vote taken in the presence of at least half of the statutory number of Deputies. The required majority in the Sejm and in the Senate, in the case of granting consent for ratification of an international agreement on the delegation of powers, shall be significantly higher than the majority required for (ordinary) legislation. It remains identical to the dimension of the qualified majority in the Sejm and is higher in relation to the Senate, compared to the majority required to enact a law amending the Constitution (Article 235(4)). From the point of view of representativeness and legitimacy, the requirements discussed above must be regarded as at least equal to those imposed to amend the Constitution. It should be emphasised that both chambers of the Parliament are equal in legislative power, as without the consent of any of the chambers there is no possibility to grant the consent. The procedure provided for in Article 90 of the Constitution strengthens the position of the Senate in the legislative process, because in practice it makes it the so-called veto player. This means that Article 121 of the Constitution, which defines the ordinary competencies of the Senate in the legislative process, is not applicable in this case (CT decision of 27 May 2003, K 11/03).

111. The referendum in view of obtaining consent for ratification of the integration agreement was held only once, to ratify the 2003 Accession Treaty. The ratification of the Lisbon Treaty took place on the basis of the statutory consent in 2008. Since the Constitution does not reserve any time limit for the President to perform the act of ratification, the Lisbon Treaty had not been ratified until 2009 (the President made the act of ratification dependent on the consent expressed in other countries, primarily on the outcome of the second referendum in Ireland).

112. The Fiscal Compact, in turn, was ratified in accordance with Article 89, i.e., after the Parliament had expressed its consent with the lower requirements. The CT in its judgment of 26 June 2013 (K 33/12) concluded that the procedure under Article 89 of the Constitution was appropriate in this case. According to the CT judgment, the content of a specific international agreement determines the choice of the procedure of granting consent. The subject matter of an international agreement may fall within the scope of the regulation of both Article 89 and Article 90 of the Constitution. In practice, this may hinder the distinction between the scope of application of both provisions. The catalogue of matters listed in Article 89(1) items 1-5 of the Constitution indicates that most of the ratified international agreements affect the way national authorities exercise their competencies. In many situations, these agreements introduce restrictions on the exercise of competency by bodies of state authority or impose obligations on them not resulting from national law (e.g., agreements on the enforcement of foreign court decisions). Moreover, this catalogue indicates that the subject matter of these agreements may be of particular constitutional importance. Yet these agreements are not subject to such a strict procedure as the agreements referred to in Article 90(1) of the Constitution. It must therefore be acknowledged that not every agreement affecting competencies of national authorities constitutes a delegation of competencies within the meaning of Article 90 of the Constitution. Only if the agreement involves delegation of the competencies of the state authorities, the special procedure laid down in Article 90 of the Polish Constitution shall apply.

§2. Kinds and Hierarchy

113. The constitutional framework gives rise to several types of international agreements, depending on how they are ratified. We can therefore distinguish between international agreements requiring ratification and those that do not. The former differ in status depending on whether prior consent for ratification is required or not.

114. According to Article 87 of the Polish Constitution, ratified international agreements are the sources of universally binding law. After their promulgation in the Journal of Laws of the RP, ratified agreements become part of the national legal order and are directly applicable unless their application depends on the enactment of a statute (Article 91(1)). These acts are assigned a sub-statutory status in the hierarchical structure of sources of law (priority of application is given to statute).

115. However, the supra-statutory status is granted to international agreements ratified with the prior consent expressed in the statute. Article 89 of the Constitution indicates which agreements require prior statutory consent for the presidential act of ratification and which agreements take precedence over statutes if the latter cannot be reconciled with the provisions of the agreement (Article 91(2)).

116. Other sources of international law, especially international agreements that do not require ratification, sometimes bear the status of internally binding law. It seems, however, that the general rule of observance of international law will be particularly meaningful in this case. Indeed, in line with the views of the CT doctrine and case law (e.g., the decision of 27 April 2005, P 1/05), the obligation to comply with international law also involves specific behaviour by public authorities. *In concreto*, therefore, an international standard can be interpreted in different ways, as generally applicable, having internal status, or as an obligation to take conventional action. In fact, these norms are not homogeneous.

Chapter 4. EU Law

§1. The Primary Law

117. The EU Treaties and other acts classified as primary EU law are recognised in the Polish Constitution as international agreements ratified upon prior consent granted in a relevant statute.

118. Their distinguishing feature, however, is the way in which consent to ratification is expressed, especially the use of Article 90 of the Polish Constitution. In the judgment of 24 November 2010 (K 32/09), when assessing the constitutionality of the Lisbon Treaty, the CT noted that the Treaty was ratified by the President of the RP with the consent granted in a statute enacted pursuant to the requirements set out in Article 90 of the Constitution. This particular ratification procedure resulted in the Treaty benefiting from a special presumption of conformity with the Constitution, since the enactment of a statute expressing consent to ratification took place after satisfying the requirements exceeding even those concerning the amendment of the Constitution. The Sejm and the Senate acted with the conviction that the Treaty was compatible with the Constitution. As a result, the presumption of constitutionality of the Treaty can only be rebutted after it has been established that there is no such interpretation of the Treaty nor the Constitution that would allow declaring the Treaty provisions to be in line with the Constitution.

§2. The Secondary Law

119. First of all, it should be noted that acts of EU law predating accession were adopted under the Treaty of Accession to the Polish legal order on the date of accession to the EU. Subsequent legal acts were issued already during the Polish membership in the Union, generally with the participation of representatives of the competent Polish authorities.

120. The Constitution, with regard to supranational legislation, employs the general category of law established by an international organisation. Pursuant to Article 91(3), this law is directly applicable, having priority in the event of a conflict with other acts. Although the doctrine attributes the sources of such law a universally binding character, the actual significance of individual sources depends on the regulations in the international agreement that establishes such an organisation (there is no doubt that the way in which EU regulations, directives and decisions, as well as recommendations and opinions, bind is different). As noted by the CT in the judgment of 11 May 2005 (K 18/04) concerning the Treaty of Accession, the systems of legal regulations coming from different legislative centres do co-exist in the territory of Poland. And they should do so through friendly interpretation and co-operative application. In another perspective, this situation shows the potential collision of norms and the priority of one of the distinguished systems.

121. This collision may be resolved in various ways. One of them is the one already indicated and described in Article 91(3). The other one was indicated by CT in its decision of 27 April 2005 (P 1/05) concerning the EAW. The Tribunal indicated three possible paths to align the European and national legal order. The fundamental value here is contained in Article 9 of the Constitution, according to which Poland observes the international law that binds it. First of all, a favourable interpretation of European law should be carried out. However, if this is not possible, the first step should be to amend the national law, including the Constitution. Ultimately, it is also possible to leave the EU.

122. In another judgment of 16 November 2011 (SK 45/09), the Tribunal examined the possibility of reviewing secondary law for its compliance with the Polish Constitution by way of a constitutional complaint. The Tribunal assumed that such a review is possible under the assumption that it is exceptional. In doing so, it relied on the jurisprudence of the German Federal Constitutional Court and assumed that as long as the EU ensures effective protection of fundamental rights equal to that resulting from the Constitution of the RP, in particular through the jurisprudence of the European Court of Justice, the CT will not examine the compatibility of secondary EU law with the Constitution. Consequently, it is for the complainant to demonstrate that the act lowers the level of protection of rights and freedoms compared to that guaranteed by the Constitution. These acts should benefit from special presumption of conformity with the Constitution.

Chapter 5. Legislation

§1. Statutory Matter

123. Statute is the instrument with the most prominent regulatory significance. Such an act may be considered both in the formal context (an act that comes into effect in a specific mode – legislative) and in the substantial one (an act containing general and abstract norms). Under the sources of law system included in the Constitution the statute is an act of parliament passed in the legislative procedure of a normative nature (general and abstract provisions) and, in principle, of an unlimited subject matter.

124. The Constitution of 1997 adopted the concept of statute as a uniform act. The Polish system of sources of law includes only the category of ordinary statutes, so there is no hierarchy of legislation in the Polish legal order that provides for organic statutes concerning system issues with higher legal validity than ordinary statutes. Even the specific mode of enactment of a statute does not grant it higher legal force. The category of ordinary statutes covers codes, budget laws, laws passed under the urgent procedure, laws initiated by citizens or laws passed as a result of a nationwide referendum, as well as a statute granting consent to ratification of an international agreement (Article 90 of the Constitution).

125. The subject matter of a statute is basically unlimited. It can be modified by supranational acts (in particular by EU regulations), due to delegation of lawmaking power. Its subject matter is also limited by the so-called regulatory matter – Articles 61(4), 112 and 123(2) of the Constitution – under which the constitutionally indicated issues should be regulated in the standing orders of the Parliament in order to avoid interference in its content by other players in the legislative process. The contents of statutes can be determined when implementing EU acts (in particular directives) and the so-called particular agreements regulating the legal status of a religious association or a church other than the Roman Catholic Church.

126. Since the subject matter of a statute is not elsewhere limited, and acts of a lower status are not of an autonomous nature (*see* Part I., Chapter 6. Executive Regulations), the category of the statutory matter assumes significance for the partition of arrangements between statute and regulation.

127. All regulatory issues are covered by the activity of the legislator (the Parliament), the statutory matter cannot be delegated to other regulatory (executive) bodies even in part, in particular repressive regulations (especially the regulation of crimes and punishments), tributary regulations, limiting the exercise of rights and freedoms guaranteed by the Constitution, as well as rules governing the judiciary. However, this does not mean that it is impossible to issue a regulation pertaining to technical matters. The principle of limiting rights and freedoms only by statutes was seriously violated during the COVID-19 pandemic. Many restrictions (like freedom of economic activity, freedom of movement, freedom of assemblies) have been introduced through regulations of Council of Ministers – not by statutes. Administrative courts usually find such prohibitions and penalties issued based on the illegality.

128. Statutes in the substantial sense contain general and abstract norms. In its decision of 14 December 2009 (K 55/07), the CT stated that the legislator should avoid regulations granting rights or imposing obligations on named private entities. However, some statutes contain norms of a singular or even individual character. As the Tribunal states, these include, *inter alia,* annual budget laws, acts expressing consent to ratification of international agreements, as well as laws on the relationship between the State and particular churches and religious associations. In addition, there is a long-standing practice of establishing laws concerning named universities, e.g., laws on the establishment of a public university or on changing the name of a public university. However, the Tribunal has not assessed the constitutionality of such practice thus far.

§2. Legislative Procedure

129. The legislative procedure in Poland is commenced with the exercise of the right of legislative initiative in the Sejm; this right cannot be exercised by submitting a bill to the Senate. According to Article 118 of the Constitution, the right of legislative initiative is vested in the Deputies (and therein in the Sejm committees or at least fifteen Deputies signing the bill, a deputy may not submit the bill individually), the Senate, the President and the Council of Ministers. A group of at least 100,000 citizens having the right to vote in elections to the Sejm is also entitled to legislative initiative. Draft laws are submitted in writing to the Speaker of the Sejm (*Marshall of the Sejm*), accompanied by justification which indicates the need and purpose of issuing the law, the current and projected state, the anticipated social, economic and legal effects, the assumptions of executive acts and indication of sources of financing, as well as a statement of compliance with EU law.

130. The systemic practice of recent years has seen the evident tendency to implement the legislative initiative primarily by Deputies, whereas governmental projects are relatively rarely submitted to the Sejm. The reason for this is fewer formal requirements for submitting a draft by Deputies – it does not have to undergo public consultations nor does it require a number of inter-ministerial arrangements and a regulatory impact assessment under the government process; the Government is also obliged to attach thorough draft executive acts to its bills, and not only their assumptions.

131. The Sejm considers bills in three readings. The right to propose modifications to the bill while it is being considered by the Sejm is vested in the sponsor of the bill, the Deputies (a group right, a Deputy cannot propose a modification on his or her own) and the Council of Ministers. The sponsor may withdraw the bill during the legislative procedure in the Sejm until the second reading of the bill is completed.

132. The first reading is carried out at a session of the Sejm or committee, but generally, the first reading is carried out in the latter. However, the essential systemic projects are considered during Sejm sittings: amendments to the Constitution, budget and tax laws, projects concerning the election of the President, election to the Sejm and the Senate and local government bodies, acts regulating the political system and jurisdiction of public authorities, as well as codes, and also those submitted by citizens. The first reading includes the sponsor's justification of the project, a debate on its general assumptions as well as questions and answers from the sponsor. The first reading in the Sejm ends with referring the proposal to the committee. Therefore, the burden of the legislative procedure lies with the Sejm committees.

133. During the second reading, the proper debate on the bill and submission of amendments and proposals take place. The third reading is connected with the final adoption of the law – it always takes place in plenary session. The Sejm adopts laws by a simple majority of votes in the presence of at least half of the statutory number of Deputies, unless the Constitution provides otherwise. The rules of procedure provide for time limits for the consecutive readings and for the Deputies to become acquainted with the bills and amendments – in practice, however, the Speaker of the Sejm, using available powers, may order three readings with almost no time interval – some laws were passed in a record-breaking single day or even several hours.[2]

134. The bill passed by the Sejm is forwarded by the Speaker of the Sejm to the Senate, where it is forwarded to the relevant Senate committees. The Senate has thirty days to adopt one of the following resolutions: adoption of the bill without changes, adoption of amendments or rejection of the bill in its entirety. The Senate's amendments must refer to the bill that has been submitted and cannot go beyond the subject matter of the act, as the institution of amendments to the bill is clearly distinguished from legislative initiative. Every matter under consideration should go through the entire legislative process, and cannot be introduced without parliamentary readings. In the case of negative Senate resolutions, the Sejm proceeds to vote. Senate's resolution rejecting the bill or an amendment proposed in Senate's resolution is considered adopted if the Sejm does not reject it by the absolute majority of votes in the presence of at least half of the statutory number of Deputies. Hence, voting in the Sejm concerns only the rejection of the Senate's position.

135. Following the Sejm's vote over the Senate's position, the bill is forwarded by the Speaker of the Sejm to the President, who orders its promulgation in the Journal of Laws of the RP. The President may submit a motion to the CT concerning the compliance of the bill with the Constitution (preventive review). The President is

2. For instance, a law increasing the tax-free amount was passed in a single day (29 Nov. 2016). The draft was sent to the Senate, and then amendments were made by the Sejm's Public Finance Committee, which the Sejm approved. It was signed by the President on the same day. Also, on 27 Jun. 2018 an amendment to the Act on the Institute of National Remembrance was passed, repealing the extremely controversial Art. 55a, which imposes criminal sanctions for attributing responsibility for the crimes of the Third German Reich to the Polish Nation.

bound by the Tribunal's decision: the President may not refuse to sign a law which has been declared compatible with the Constitution by the Tribunal and is obliged to refuse to sign a law which has been deemed unconstitutional. The Constitution also provides for a situation in which the unconstitutionality concerns only individual provisions of a statute. Subsequently, after obtaining the opinion of the Speaker of the Sejm, the President shall either sign the bill without the provisions deemed unconstitutional or return it to the Sejm in order to eliminate the inconsistency and adapt it to the Tribunal's judgment. These solutions do not apply if the unconstitutional provisions are inextricably linked to the entire law. Such inconsistencies shall then extend to the entire bill, and the President cannot sign it.

136. The President also holds the right of suspension veto, i.e., right to a reasoned request to reconsider the bill in the Sejm. This procedure may be used if no motion has been filed to the CT. It is indicated that the reasons for using veto should be of a different nature than the unconstitutional nature of the legislation (political, social, ethical, economic). The veto raised by the President may be overturned by the Sejm, which, by the majority of three-fifth votes in the presence of at least half of the statutory number of Deputies, passes the bill anew. Then the President signs the bill within seven days and orders its promulgation. If the law is passed again, the President has no right to refer it to the CT in the course of preventive review. However, the President may use the mode of repressive review.

137. When the Sejm's term of office comes to an end, the suspension veto exercised by the President may turn into a decisive one, combined with the failure to implement the law. It is the outcome of the principle of discounting the activities of the Parliament being adopted. According to this principle, all motions considered by these bodies, especially legislative ones, are discontinued with the end of the term of the Sejm and the Senate. Unfinished proceedings are considered unresolved. Therefore, if the President submits a veto just before the end of the term of office (the day before the new Sejm convenes) bearing in mind the twenty-one-day deadline, the Sejm cannot restart the proceedings.

138. The Constitution also provides for special modes within the legislative procedure. These include the urgent mode, the budgetary mode, an act granting consent to the ratification of an international agreement under which Poland delegates part of the powers of its bodies in certain matters and a statute amending the Constitution.

139. The urgent mode is initiated by the Council of Ministers and concerns only the bills adopted by it. This mode cannot be applied to draft tax laws, laws on the election of the President, the Sejm, the Senate and local self-government bodies, laws regulating the political system and jurisdiction of public authorities, and codes as well. The deadlines for the Senate (fourteen days) and for the President (seven days) are shortened under this mode. It is not used frequently – due to Speaker's power to shorten terms within the legislative procedure in the Sejm, based on authorisation to do so prescribed in standing orders. An interesting tendency has been observed in Polish parliamentary practice, especially since 2015, to pass bills very quickly, without initiating the urgent mode, and without any reasonable urgent need. Such rapid proceedings are justified only by political reasons.

140. The budget mode is related to the adoption of the Budget, the interim budget and amendments thereto. The Budget is adopted for one calendar year (1 January–31 December). According to Article 221, the exclusive right of legislative initiative for the Council of Ministers is provided for in relation to the draft of the aforesaid acts and the statute on contracting the public debt, as well as a statute granting financial guarantees by the State. This means that no other body can effectively propose such a bill. It should be stressed, however, that the budgetary procedure concerns only the Budget, the interim budget and amendments thereto. The other two acts (on public debt and on the granting of financial guarantees by the State) are adopted under the ordinary legislative procedure.

141. Regarding the Budget, the Constitution provides for the obligation on the Government to submit a draft by 30 September of the year preceding the budget year, i.e., no later than three months before the commencement of the fiscal year (Article 222). In exceptional instances, the draft may be submitted later. Under the budgetary mode, the powers of the Senate and the President are modified. The Senate may adopt the Budget without amendments or adopt amendments to it, but cannot reject it. In this case, the Senate should work out its position within twenty days of the bill being submitted. The President has seven days to sign the Budget, but he cannot veto it. The President may, however, ask the CT to examine the compatibility of these laws with the Constitution before signing them. The Tribunal has limited time and must decide on the constitutionality of the Budget within two months of the motion being submitted. The work on the Budget in the Sejm and the Senate should be completed within four months. This period begins on the day the draft budget is submitted to the Sejm and ends on the day the law adopted by the Sejm and the Senate is presented to the President for signature. Failure to meet this deadline may result in the President requesting that the term of the Sejm be shortened. The President may do so within fourteen days from the expiration of the deadline within which the bill should be signed. It is not allowed to do that after this period. If the Budget Law is not passed on the day of the beginning of the financial year (1 January), the Government runs the State's financial economy on the basis of the submitted draft.

142. A different mode of enactment applies to bills expressing consent to the conclusion of an international agreement delegating powers of state authorities (*see* Part I., Chapter 3., §1. The Treaty-Making Power).

Chapter 6. Executive Regulations

§1. Characteristics

143. An act related to statute in an almost genetic way is a regulation. According to Article 92 of the Constitution, regulations shall be issued on the basis of specific authorisation contained in, and for the purpose of implementation of, statutes by the organs specified in the Constitution. The authorisation shall specify the organ appropriate to issue a regulation and the scope of matters to be regulated as well as guidelines concerning the provisions of such an act. An organ authorised to issue a regulation shall not delegate its competency to another organ (prohibition of subdelegation).

144. Regulation consists of universally binding, general and abstract norms. It is not an autonomous act, as it requires a statutory authorisation in each case, nor is it an independent act, as it serves to implement the statute. This act is closely connected with the statute it implements. It performs a servant role in relation to it. It has a separate object of regulation from the statute (it cannot regulate the same issues and in the same way as the authorising statute, it cannot rephrase its provisions), although it is connected to it in terms of competency and function. It governs organisational and technical issues which are not of primary social importance and which may be subject to frequent changes, but are necessary for the proper functioning of the statute.

145. The institution of executive regulations has been elaborated widely in the CT case law. In the decision of 29 May 2009 (P 58/07) the Tribunal stated that a regulation may be issued only on the basis of an explicit, precise statutory authorisation and only within the limits of it. Such authorisation needs to be detailed in terms of its subject matter; i.e., it must specify the authority competent to issue the regulation and the scope of the cases submitted for regulation. It has to be detailed also in terms of its content, i.e., it must indicate, in positive or negative form, the guidelines for the content of the act. Guidelines mean instructions concerning the act, setting out the directions of substantive solutions; basic assumptions; courses of action; directives; indicators concerning what the content of the regulation should aim at (positive guidelines) or exclude certain solutions (negative guidelines). They should be of substantive character (the matter and the shape of the future executive regulation). The substantive detail of the guidelines is gradual depending on the regulated matter. The minimum content of the guidelines is not constant. They ought to be most detailed in matters concerning the legal situation of citizens. Each separate matter requires separate guidelines.

146. Consequently, the essence of the solution adopted in Article 92(1) is that all fundamental issues concerning future lawmaking should be determined in the delegating act, i.e., in the statute. The regulation must serve the purpose of the statute. Authorisation cannot be founded on a presumption or on a purposeful interpretation. Provisions conferring legislative competency shall be interpreted strictly and literally. The authorisation may be either optional (entitling to issue an act) or obligatory (obliging to issue a regulation). It is constitutionally inadmissible to formulate any authorisation which, in essence, does not authorise the issuance of an executive act to implement the statute, but to regulate the entire complex of issues which have no direct regulations or guidelines in the text of the statute.

147. The Tribunal also points out that the provisions of the regulation lay down the conditions for the application of the rules set out in the statute itself and make them more specific in so far as the legislature has not done so on account of their secondary meaning. The regulation is therefore a functional supplement to the statute. It serves as a development of the issues governed by an act of parliament. However, the statute should give the authorised body certain autonomy in regulating the matter covered by the regulation. It is important for the entity issuing the regulation to be able to correctly read the intentions of the legislator on the basis of guidelines contained in the authorisation.

148. From a theoretical point of view, a regulation is an act originating from the executive bodies, which bear political accountability. The bodies that may be authorised to issue it are clearly indicated in the text of the Constitution. These are: the departmental/ministry minister (a minister 'without a portfolio' cannot issue regulations), the Prime Minister, the Government, the chairman of the committee indicated in the law and being a member of the Government (although this category is practically defunct), the President, the National Broadcasting Council (KRRiT) (in this case, one must bear in mind the doubts as to whether this body should be classified as an executive power). The Constitution prohibits sub-delegation; the law-making power may not be delegated to another body. However, the issuance of a regulation by a deputy minister in lieu of a minister is not considered violation of this prohibition. It also appears that sub-delegation cannot be allowed by way of statute. The ban seems to concern delegation of powers by the body itself, as well as under the act.

149. A special type of regulation deviating from the classical structure provided for in Article 92 of the Polish Constitution is the regulation on the introduction of extraordinary measures (linked to state of emergency, state of natural disaster, martial law – *see* Part V. Extraordinary Measures: Martial Law, a State of Emergency or a State of Natural Disaster). In formal terms, they are still regulations, but their contents, on the other hand, include updating the obligations and competencies granted to specific entities in the act on a given state of emergency, as well as the act of selecting those that are updated upon the introduction of that state of emergency. In this context, they are identified with the acts of applying the law, and more specifically the Constitution. This type of regulation is heterogeneous in nature – on the one hand, it bears the characteristics of a regulation; after all, it is issued on the basis of statute – but its execution is different (Article 228(2) of the Polish Constitution). Occasionally, it is explicitly stated that the authorisation to issue regulations results directly from the Constitution. On the other hand, it is an act of proclamation of a state of emergency, which produces legal effects described in the act. Those regulations are described as specific legal acts, having at the same time the character of an individual act (it establishes a specific state of emergency) and a common one (it generally and abstractly defines extraordinary measures concerning the status of an individual).

§2. Limits: Delegation of Legislative Power

150. The Polish Constitution does not provide for the possibility of delegating legislative power, whereas the Small Constitution of 1992 did. Upon well-grounded request of the Council of Ministers, the Sejm, by virtue of a law adopted by the absolute majority of Deputies' votes, could authorise it to issue regulations with the force of statute. In practice, this institution was not applied.

151. The Constitution of 1997 exclusively entrusts the legislative authority (the Sejm with the participation of the Senate) with the process of adopting acts with the force of statute. The exception, however, concerns the so-called exceptional legislation, i.e., regulations with statutory force (Article 234). These are acts originating from the executive and intended to ensure continuity of the State's activities in a crisis. They are issued during martial law if the Sejm is not able to convene. They are issued by the President at the request of the Council of Ministers. These regulations are subject to approval by the Sejm at its next sitting. It is therefore impossible to describe it as classic delegation of legislative power.

Chapter 7. Local Law

152. Enactments of local law enjoy the constitutional status of sources of universally binding law (Article 87(2) of the Polish Constitution). However, their area of validity is limited to the territorial jurisdiction of the constituting authority.

153. On the basis of and within the limits of the authorisations specified by statute, local self-government bodies and local government administration bodies establish local legal enactments binding in the area where these bodies operate (Article 94 of the Polish Constitution). Essentially, these enactments are secondary legislation, although the authorisation to issue them does not have to be as detailed as in the case of regulations.

154. Enactments of local law should not be equated with the delegation of law-making powers. Local self-government is autonomous in this respect. There is a particular relationship between statute and acts of local law. In its judgment of 8 July 2003 (P 10/02), the CT allowed even in statute the use of the carte blanche technique (the authorised body fills it in itself) in repressive regulations, provided, however, that statute provides for minor penalties (all forms of restriction of personal freedom by means other than included in statute are constitutionally excluded); and the regulation comes from bodies endowed with democratic legitimacy established by universal and direct elections. The statute must also clearly express the will to penalise behaviour prohibited by law enforcement regulations, and the scope of the referral is aligned with the limits of the legislative powers of public authorities stipulated by the Constitution.

Chapter 8. Sources of Internal Law: Characteristics

155. The system of internal law acts – namely, acts binding only in the sphere of internal subordination – is regulated by the Constitution only to limited extent. Acts listed in Article 93(1) of the Polish Constitution constitute the core of this system, according to which resolutions of the Council of Ministers and orders of the Prime Minister and ministers shall be of an internal character and shall bind only those organisational units subordinate to the organ which issues such act. Orders are issued only on the basis of statute. They cannot serve as basis for decisions issued to citizens, legal persons and other entities. Resolutions and orders are subject to scrutiny regarding their compliance with universally binding law. In its judgment of 1 December (K 21/98), the CT ruled that there is no constitutional prohibition for statutory provisions to authorise other entities to pass orders or resolutions, or even acts under different designation, that correspond with the characteristics of an internal law act (e.g., State Electoral Commission resolutions addressed to electoral bodies). Thus, the system of internal law is of an open nature; however, the Tribunal decided in the above-mentioned ruling that all acts of an internal nature must fit into the model defined in Article 93 of the Polish Constitution.

156. Acts of internal law can concern different areas of regulation. Three basic scopes can be distinguished here: organisation of an entity, including authorities enjoying autonomy; procedural issues, as well as proper (ethical) performance of its tasks by members of the collective entity (e.g., codes of ethics). However, such an act cannot assume an interpretive role.

157. It is not easy to identify the appropriate form of source of internal law in practice. Article 93 of the Constitution indicates two basic types of acts: resolutions and orders. It does not define them, and at the same time various acts with different names appear in practice, e.g., regulations, statutes, ordinances.

Part II. Form of Government

Chapter 1. Democracy

§1. Introduction

158. Democracy is first and foremost related to the principle of sovereignty of the Nation, as described in Article 4 of the Constitution, and embodied in the principle of the democratic rule of law (*see* General Introduction, §2., II., V. National Sovereignty and Forms of Democracy).

159. Under the Constitution of 1997, democracy is classically perceived as a form of governance in the State, based on the assumption of equality and freedom of all citizens who are guaranteed influence on decision-making in the State, either directly or through their elected representatives. Additionally, they enjoy the right to monitor and scrutinise persons exercising public powers. The Constitution not only promotes the representative formula of democracy but also provides for the possibility of expressing the will directly by the Nation in the form of a referendum and a citizens' initiative. The principle of the democratic form of exercising power is implemented through such constitutional principles and rules as: political pluralism, principles of electoral law, elections to the Parliament and other representative bodies, as well as mechanisms of mutual scrutiny and balance of power. In turn, the supervision and monitoring of the exercise of power is guaranteed at the constitutional level through the right to public information, the functioning of free media and civic society institutions. Those guarantees also come in the form of individual rights (in particular the right to vote, the right of association, the right to information and freedom of expression).

160. In 1989 it was assumed that democracy cannot be limited to majority formulas alone, and it is widely acknowledged that it needs to protect minorities as well. An expression of this assumption is found in the Constitution's adoption of the principle of equality before the law and prohibition of discrimination. From the political point of view, liberal understanding of democracy is particularly connected with political pluralism and freedom of operation of political parties.

§2. POLITICAL PARTIES

161. Political parties play a significant role within the Polish constitutional system. They shape the political system and ensure its proper functioning. Persons affiliated to the parties express their political will, become part of the authorities exercising power in the State and hold the highest offices. Therefore, political parties represent the basic principle of freedom of association on the one hand, and the creation of a political system on the other. Pluralism, including the freedom of establishment and operation of political parties, is necessary for the proper functioning of a political system.

162. According to Article 11 of the Constitution, the RP shall ensure freedom for the creation and functioning of political parties. These shall be founded on the principle of voluntariness and upon the equality of Polish citizens, and their purpose shall be to influence the formulation of the policy of the State by democratic means. Article 13 specifies the types of political parties and other organisations existence of which is prohibited (*see* General Introduction, §2., V. National Sovereignty and Forms of Democracy). Consequently, this legal rule prohibits promotion of values most devastating towards the democratic system.

163. Political parties are also governed by the provisions of Article 58, which guarantees the freedom of association to everyone. However, the formations whose purposes or activities oppose the Constitution or the law in force shall be prohibited. If this is the case, the courts shall decide on the refusal to register or on the crossing-out an association from the party registry if its activities do not comply with the law. Statutes shall specify types of associations requiring court registration, a procedure for such a registration and the forms of supervision of such associations. These types of associations encompass political parties.

164. In respect to the control over political parties it should be referred to Article 188, that states that the CT shall adjudicate *inter alia* regarding the compatibility of the purposes or activities of political parties with the Constitution.

165. The CT dealt with the problem of political parties several times. In the judgment of 8 March 2000 (Pp 1/99) CT highlighted the position and function of political parties. The Tribunal stated that a party is a form of implementation of the Polish citizens' freedom of association. Simultaneously, due to its ability to impact and shape the State's policy, it constitutes an element of the State's political system. Political parties are treated as important and constitutionally indispensable elements of the liberal democratic rule of law. Their main function is to influence the state policy, which is guaranteed by the relevant constitutional and statutory regulations. Both the place where the provisions concerning the parties are located and their content show that these formations are ranked as the 'basic institutions of the public political life'. As stated by the CT, the principle of political pluralism (Article 11) is an inviolable principle of the system because of the importance and the function of a party in a democratic state.

166. Further, the CT addressed the problem of interference with the internal structure of the political party by the state authority. In this respect, the Tribunal referred to its decision of 24 April 1996 (W 14/95), issued prior-constitution, and stated that the constitutional right of citizens to associate into political parties does not exclude the legislator's option to establish either its limits or the legal procedure to be followed. This is because freedoms of citizens are not absolute and may be subject to limitations. Those limits may be laid down both in political parties' or public interest, in order to guarantee a democratic system of government. Additionally, the internal organisation, i.e., the membership and the structure, is to be based on the principles of equality and voluntariness, namely on the democratic principles. Violation of one of these rules would not allow classifying a given social organisation as a political party.

167. Thus, democratic principles also refer to the internal affairs. Moreover, they regard the purpose of the establishment of a party, its activities, the system of authorities and the issues related to the membership. Therefore, in a party statute or other documents equivalent to it, a party ought to clarify its position in a political system and its influence on the state policy. As a consequence, the CT indicated that the postulate of 'democratic methods' does not only regard the 'external' activities of a party, i.e., essentially the sphere of its political activity, but also the 'internal' activities relating to its structure and the rules of membership.

168. Nevertheless, the CT stated that although the internal organisation of a party might be undemocratic, the institution might still fulfil its constitutional role. Therefore, the freedom to determine the internal structures and the principles of functioning of a party cannot be limited as long as this party acts constitutionally or as long as it does not exclude democratic methods to shape the state policy.

169. The Constitution provides for transparency of party financing. Given the public funding model of the party, it is assumed that it may not engage in economic activities. Income from property is also subject to far-reaching restrictions and can only originate from: interest on funds accumulated in bank accounts and deposits; trading in Treasury bonds and Treasury bills; sale of its assets; and sale of so-called party gadgets. In addition, a party may rent its real estate and premises only as Deputies' and Senators' offices, as well as the offices of self-governmental councillors. Parties should accumulate funds on bank accounts and are forbidden to conduct public fundraising events. The legislator allowed political parties to take out bank loans for statutory purposes. The restrictions also apply to the use of party assets. It can only be used for statutory or charitable purposes.

170. Political parties are obliged to report annual financial information, especially about the subsidy received and the expenses incurred from it. This information is submitted to the State Electoral Commission. If the information is not submitted and if irregularities are found in the spending of funds, such a political party loses the subsidy for one year.

§3. REFERENDUM

171. The Constitution of 1997 provides for a referendum to be held at national and local level.

172. Pursuant to Article 125 of the Constitution, a nationwide referendum may be held in respect to matters of particular importance to the State. It may be ordered by the Sejm by the absolute majority of votes in the presence of at least half of the statutory number of Deputies or by the President with the consent of the Senate expressed by the absolute majority of votes in the presence of at least half of the statutory number of Senators. The act ordering a referendum does not qualify as a normative act and is therefore not subject to review by the CT regarding its constitutionality. A referendum is binding when more than half of those entitled to vote have taken part in it. A non-binding result has no legal significance, but can undoubtedly have political impact.

173. A matter of particular importance for the State, which is to be voted upon in the referendum, must meet two criteria. First, the issue must be of particular social importance, and second, the issue must be relevant for the entire State. The latter criterion, however, cannot be limited to state matters defined as a group of institutions and people acting on behalf of the State. The referendum is a form of direct exercise of power by the Nation, and it ought to serve this very purpose. Therefore, issues voted upon may include an important matter for all citizens or a significant part of them, but one that is directly related to the interests of the State as a whole. Traditionally, the concept is clarified by indicating the following subject matter of a nationwide referendum: constitutional regulations; state system issues, such as self-government reform; consent to the use of modern technology, such as the production of atomic energy; freedom of people's moral behaviour – protection of life conceived or marriage of same-sex people; and the resolution of specific public matters. Other possibilities include: matter of the independent existence of the State; territorial changes; acceptance or rejection of an international agreement; approval of the function of the Head of State, e.g., extension of the term of office; economic decisions, e.g., privatisation, enfranchisement.

174. The Polish Constitution also provides for two specific cases of a nationwide referendum which differ procedurally. The first one concerns the consent to ratify an international agreement, under which Poland may delegate the competency of state authority bodies in certain matters to an international organisation or body (Article 90). The mode of expression of such consent for ratification may be either statutory or through a referendum. The resolution on the selection of mode is adopted by the Sejm by the absolute majority of votes in the presence of at least half of the statutory number of Deputies. The difference here lies in the indication of the body entitled to decide on the admissibility of the procedure of consent for ratification of an international agreement expressed in the referendum. Then the referendum may be ordered by the Sejm or by the President upon the consent of the Senate on the basis of Article 125 of the Polish Constitution (*see* Chapter 3., §1. The Treaty-Making Power).

175. The second exceptional case is a referendum on the amendment of the Constitution. Article 235(6) of the Constitution allows for the possibility of a nationwide referendum if the Act on the amendment of the Constitution concerns the provisions of Chapters I, II or XII. Entities holding the right of political initiative (at least one-fifth of the statutory number of Deputies, the Senate or the President) may request a referendum to be held on its approval within forty-five days from the date of the adoption of statute by the Senate. These entities turn to the Speaker of the Sejm, who immediately orders a referendum to be held within sixty days of the date of the request. Accordingly, referendum can only be ordered by the Speaker of the Sejm. An amendment to the Constitution shall be adopted if majority of voters is in favour of the amendment. In this case, the turnout requirement for a binding referendum result has therefore been abolished. It is worth noting that it makes it impossible to adopt a completely new Constitution, although a revision of the Constitution should be allowed (change of the political system of the state).

176. In any case, the validity of a nationwide referendum is determined by the SC.

177. Basically, there are no temporal restrictions as regards the possibility of holding a referendum. It can be ordered at any time, even immediately after the previous referendum on the same issue. A nationwide referendum cannot be held only during a period of introduction of extraordinary measures and within ninety days after it has ended (Article 228(7) of the Constitution).

178. At the local level, members of a self-governing community may decide, by means of a referendum, matters concerning their community, including the dismissal of an organ of local government established by direct election (Article 170 of the Constitution). This regulation, considered together with Article 62 of the Constitution, grants the right to participate in a local referendum to every adult member of the local self-government community who holds Polish citizenship, has full public rights, including electoral ones and is not incapacitated. This person should demonstrate permanent residency on the territory of a given local government unit. It can be deduced explicitly from this regulation that foreigners have been excluded from participation in a local referendum. However, the issue of the right to participate in local elections of citizens of EU Member States should be qualified differently. In this context, extension of the right to participate in a local referendum should also be considered – Article 170 of the Constitution determines the participation in a referendum of members of self-governing community, which consists of all residents according to Article 16 of the Constitution.

179. In the light of the presented constitutional regulations, we can organise the institution of a referendum, taking into account its territorial range, to the national one – covering the whole country and the local one – conducted on the territory of a given local self-government unit.

180. The Constitution of 1997 does not recognise the institution of an obligatory referendum. A nationwide referendum, regardless of the matter it concerns, is always free in terms of participation. Nevertheless, there is a solution which provides for the possibility (an ordinary nationwide referendum) or obligation (a constitutional referendum) to call for the referendum if an application for one is submitted.

181. As far as the subject matter is considered, we can divide the referenda into legislative, constitutional and resolution-making ones. The legislative referendum concerns matters that can be regulated by statute. The constitutional referendum, in the current political reality, may concern matters regulated in Chapters I, II and XII of the Constitution. The scope of the resolution-making referendum is related to this institution of direct democracy, effective at the local level in all areas where a resolution may be adopted by the bodies of individual local self-government units.

182. It should be underlined that generally the referendum does not replace existing appropriate form of regulation on the particular matter. With regard to the constitutional matter, the already enacted law on amending the Constitution is approved. Whereas with regard to the matter of a statute and a resolution by way of a referendum, an obligation arises for the bodies to implement appropriate procedures aimed at facilitating the adoption of the statute or the resolution. The result of the referendum replaces the form of statute only in the event of expressing consent to ratify an international agreement referred to in Article 90 of the Constitution.

§4. Other Forms of Direct Democracy

183. In Article 118(2) the Constitution grants the right of legislative initiative to a group of at least 100,000 citizens entitled to vote in elections to the Sejm. When submitting a bill to the Sejm, the sponsors also present the financial consequences of its implementation (Article 118(3) of the Constitution). The right of citizens is a right equivalent to the right of the other subjects of the legislative initiative.

184. Citizens exercise their right of legislative initiative by signing a letter supporting the bill. The support for the bill should amount to at least 100,000 signatures, which is considered to be a reasonable threshold. Only citizens who have the right to vote in elections to the Sejm, i.e., in accordance with Article 62 of the Constitution, may be involved in exercising their right of legislative initiative if, not later than on the day of voting, they are at least 18 years old and have not been incapacitated or deprived of public or electoral rights by virtue of a final court decision.

185. However, the right of initiative enjoyed by the citizens is limited. The bill being prepared may concern matters for which the Constitution does not reserve the exclusive competency of other entities. These restrictions apply to the matters set out in Articles 221 and 235 of the Constitution (Budget and constitutional amendments) and, as a matter of custom, also include laws expressing consent to ratification of an international agreement, or laws regulating relations between the state and churches.

186. Polish law also envisages various forms of consultations as a separate institution of direct democracy. In Poland, this form remains outside the Constitution and results from statutory regulations. Consultations consist in expressing an opinion on the presented matter. However, they are not of a binding character. A participant may present his or her own comments, postulates or suggested solutions. It pertains to specific social groups (e.g., a trade union organisation based on Article 19 and 19(1) of the Act of 23 May 1991 on Trade Unions) or local communities (e.g., based on Article 5a of the Act of 8 March 1990 on Municipal Self-Government).

187. Lobbying can also be regarded as a form similar in effect, as it may also be a form in which citizens express their opinions. Lobbying in Poland is regulated by the Act of 7 July 2005 on Lobbying Activities in the Lawmaking Process and is treated as actions of professional lobbyists aimed at influencing the lawmaking or the decisions of the State, local self-government or other bodies. Legal lobbying is strictly regulated in its forms and must meet rigorous requirements regarding transparency. A distinction is made to differentiate from the right of petition, which can be used by everyone as described in Article 63 of the Constitution.

188. It should be noted that direct democracy in Poland is widely treated as a way of democratically influencing decisions in public matters. In its judgment of 10 July 2008 (P 15/08), the CT stressed that assemblies are an essential element of the democratic expression of public opinion, providing an opportunity to influence the political process, allowing criticism and protest, thus forming a part of the process of deliberative direct democracy. Spontaneous assemblies also serve the purpose of effective social control.

Chapter 2. The Legislature

§1. The Organs of State

I. Bicameralism

189. Polish Parliament is a bicameral one and consists of two chambers, the Sejm and the Senate. Bicameralism is well rooted in the Polish political tradition; when Poland was politically independent, especially in the years 1918–1939, the Parliament also consisted of these two chambers. The Parliament lost both its status as an organ of power under the socialists' reign, as it was actually exercised by the communist party, as well as lost its structure, abandoning the tradition of bicameralism. However, as early as 1989, the Round Table reinstated the second chamber of Parliament and held elections to the newly constituted Senate. Its composition was shaped following fully democratic elections – unlike the elections to the Sejm, arranged according to the rules set by the Government, under which only 35% of the seats were filled freely (all those seats went to the opposition). For this historical reason, the term of office of the Sejm has a different designation than that of the Senate – it is continuously numbered from the first formation of a chamber elected entirely freely. Thus, the first term of the Senate fell between 1989 and 1991, while the Sejm's did not begin until 1991.

190. Nonetheless, the role of the systemic status of the Senate was not entirely clear from the very beginning, both in relation to the Sejm and the other governing bodies. Polish Constitutional Law determines that, although both chambers exercise legislative power, we are dealing with a model of a differentiated and asymmetric two-chamber system in Poland, with the Sejm holding much more functions and having more competencies than the Senate. This manifests itself in all three functions of the Parliament: legislative, scrutiny and formative (of appointing public officials). The Senate's legislative functions are performed through legislative initiative and the right of veto over laws being passed by the Sejm – but the Sejm may reject them by the absolute majority of votes in the presence of at least half of the statutory number of members. The Senate has no scrutiny over the Government at all. However, although it is mandatory to obtain the Senate's consent to appoint many other high-level state officials selected by the Sejm, the Senate does not participate in the appointment of the Government.

191. The Senate's limited rank does not correlate with the way it is formed. The Senate is elected by universal suffrage and at the same time as the Sejm. The mandate of both chambers and their respective terms of office are then identical.

II. Electoral System

A. General Introduction

192. The Constitution states that elections to the Sejm shall be universal, equal, direct, proportional and shall be conducted by secret ballot (Article 96(2)). As regards elections to the Senate, Article 97(2) states that they shall be universal, direct and shall be conducted by secret ballot. As such, there is no constitutional guarantee of equal suffrage in Senate elections, and it takes the form of majority voting, not the proportional one.

193. On the other hand, as is also stressed in the studies of constitutional law, the proportionality of parliamentary elections cannot be waived, not even in part, e.g., in favour of a mixed system (known, e.g., from the elections to German Bundestag).

194. Among the principles of the law on parliamentary elections there was also a formulation of the principle of freedom of choice as it was particularly important in the context of the political transformation of 1989. As a result of the Round Table agreements, a so-called contractual Sejm was formed, in which the previous authorities had a guaranteed percentage share, while the elections to the Senate were already free – which was reflected in the text of the electoral law and in the Small Constitution of 1992. Under the 1997 Constitution, however, it has been emphasised that the process relies on the principle of political pluralism and freedom of political parties, which implies freedom of elections on its own.

195. The rules, mode and organisation of elections have been unified and regulated by the Electoral Code since 2011.

B. The Principles of the Election Process

1. The Principle of Universality of Elections

196. This principle stipulates that citizens must be provided with the widest possible access to participate in the elections – both to choose (vote) and to run in the electoral campaign as a candidate. In addition, this principle eliminates the possibility of arbitrary exclusion of citizens from participation in the elections for reasons irrelevant from the point of view of the voting process. The conditions of participation, known as censuses, can therefore only be objective and formulated based on the most important criteria concerning voter characteristics. In Polish law these are age and citizenship.

197. The active right to vote is guaranteed by Article 62 of the Constitution, according to which a Polish citizen has the right to elect Deputies and Senators if he or she turns 18 on the day of vote at the latest. This right is not granted to persons who are incapacitated or deprived of public or electoral rights by a final court judgment.

198. Passive electoral right (the right to stand as a candidate in elections) is defined in Article 99 of the Constitution. According to this provision, every citizen having the right to vote, who, no later than on the day of the elections, has attained the age of 21 years, shall be eligible to be elected to the Sejm (Article 99(1) of the Constitution). In case of the Senate, the age requirement is set at 30 years (Article 99(2)).

199. Since the adoption of the amendment to the Constitution on 7 May 2009, no person sentenced to imprisonment by a final judgment for an intentional indictable offence may be elected to the Sejm or the Senate nor for the office of the President (Article 99(3)).

200. Only Polish citizens can take part in parliamentary elections – it is treated as a consequence of principle of National sovereignty and status of Parliament as a representation of the Nation. The Electoral Code, on the other hand, specifies that citizens of EU Member States also have the right to vote in local self-government elections, provided that they reside permanently in the commune, district and voivodeship where the elections are held. In these local self-governmental bodies Deputies represent a local community and all habitants – not only the citizens.

201. Electoral law creates a system of guarantees for the implementation of the principle of universality through instruments of protection against arbitrary exclusion of voters (*see* Part II., Chapter 2., §2., II., D. Voters).

2. The Principle of Directness

202. It means that the voter casts his/her vote directly for the candidate of choice – without appointing any intermediaries, i.e., electors. This principle applies to the act of voting itself – but also to the way in which the voter casts a vote for a particular person. The principle of directness is implemented in full in majority elections (to the Senate), while in case of proportional elections to the Sejm, the voter casts a vote for a candidate on the electoral list and the vote is counted as cast for a certain list (electoral committee), and indicating a candidate means a voter's preference as to the order in which the mandate is to be allocated within that list, provided that the candidate is eligible for the distribution of seats (exceeds the electoral threshold).

203. The issue of directness is related to the institution of voting by proxy, acceptable within the Polish electoral system as an exception to the principle of voting in person. The elderly (over 75 years of age) and the disabled may vote with the aid of a proxy; a representative's authorisation (in a special form) may be accepted only from one person, and – if one of them is a close relative of the representative – from two.

204. Another form of voting allowed under the Polish electoral law is postal voting – initially allowed only among voters exercising their right outside the RP, but in 2014 it became available to all voters for the next few years. Yet, since 2018 it has been limited to the disabled only.

205. Again, in 2020 there was a change in the date and mode of conducting the election of the President of Poland because of the COVID-19 pandemic. Initially scheduled for 10 May, the vote – ordered entirely as a postal voting (all-postal voting) – did not take place, but the law was adopted at the beginning of June 2020, according to which all voters who express their will to vote by post, in particular those subject to quarantine, may do so. Elections were held in this mode at the end of June (second round in July) 2020.

3. The Principle of Equality

206. The principle of equality has a formal and a material aspect. Formally, it means that each voter has an equal number of votes. Under the current wording of the Electoral Code, both in elections to the Sejm and to the Senate each voter has one vote (under the previous legal regime, from 1989 to 2011 voters had several (from two to three), and as of 2001 – four votes, depending on the size of the constituency when electing to the Senate).

207. Material equality means that the voting power of all eligible voters is the same. Consequently, the ratio between the support expressed for the committees and the number of seats obtained is maintained. It is guaranteed primarily by: division into constituencies and uniform standard of representation, which determines the number of voters per seat, as well as uniform and neutral rules of election campaign for committees.

208. The constitutional principle of equality of women and men has also been regulated separately in the electoral process. The 2011 Electoral Code provides for so-called electoral quotas, stating that the number of women cannot be lower than 35% of the total number of candidates on the list and the number of men cannot be lower than 35% of the total number of candidates on the list either. There were 130 women in the Sejm (from 2015 to 2019, the same amount in 2019 elections), which gives only about 28%. In the Senate, however, it was only 14 women per 100 Senators, this number grew into 28% in 2019 elections.

4. The Principle of Proportionality

209. According to this principle, the number of votes cast is proportional to the number of seats obtained. The principle is implemented with regard to elections to the Sejm, which are held in multi-mandate constituencies. The d'Hondt method has been applied in Poland for thirty years (with exceptions in 1991 and 2001 elections), according to which the number of votes cast by election committees is divided by successive natural numbers, and the obtained quotients are counted in sequence, entitling candidates to get the seats (each election list receives the number of seats indicated by the highest quotients obtained put in order to exhaust the number of seats in the constituency).

210. This rule applies to elections to the Sejm, the European Parliament and certain collective bodies of local self-government.

211. Elections to the Senate are held in single-mandate constituencies and of course, such character is also applicable to the elections of the President of the RP and of the heads (mayors and presidents) in local self-government. They are therefore majority elections, and elections to the Senate are held according to the ordinary majority of votes system, while the elections of the President and the municipal body are held according to the system of absolute majority.

5. Secret Ballot Principle

212. This principle is intended to ensure the freedom of choice. It is guaranteed by the technical conditions at the polling station, but it is also linked to the ban on publishing polls twenty-four hours prior and on the day of the election.

C. Candidates, Electoral Campaign

213. As stated in Article 100 of the Constitution, candidates for Deputies and Senators may be nominated by political parties or voters – they do so through electoral committees (in the case of parties, the role of the committee is played by the bodies of these parties entitled to represent them). The committees begin their activities after being notified to the State Electoral Commission. The committees register lists of candidates in electoral constituencies – in each constituency one list of candidates may be registered, provided that at least 5,000 voters residing permanently in the constituency have voiced their support. Since 2011, the Polish Electoral Law requires that the list of candidates must include at least 35% of women and 35% of men (electoral quota).

214. In elections to the Senate, candidates are also nominated by electoral committees – provided that the signatures of 2,000 voters from the constituency are obtained and each committee nominates only one candidate.

215. However, the voters' right to nominate candidates to the Sejm is quite ephemeral due to the adopted electoral system: the proportional system and the method of calculating the seats for larger committees, i.e., the d'Hondt method and the election threshold: only those committees that have exceeded 5% of voters' support nationwide participate in the distribution of seats in the Sejm; for election coalitions this threshold stands at 8% (only national minority committees are exempt from the obligation to exceed 5% – in practice, they are implemented only by the German minority).

216. When the mandate of a Deputy (*a Member of the Sejm*) expires, the composition of the Parliament is supplemented by the next candidate from the same committee list, according to the number of votes cast. In the event of the vacancy of a Senator's seat, supplementary elections are held.

217. The election campaign is subject to strict regulations, both in terms of conducting the process and financing it. The Electoral Code defines impermissible methods of electoral agitation (e.g., it is forbidden to conduct such agitation in schools, workplaces, offices and military units), the access of election committees to air time in public media is strictly regulated. The rules of broadcasting election programmes free of charge in these media outlets are also defined for election committees that have registered a certain number of lists in their constituencies. During the election campaign there is also a special procedure for pursuing claims related to the dissemination of false information about candidates – such a claim is examined by the court within twenty-four hours, an appeal is also considered within the next twenty-four hours, and an entity found guilty of disseminating false information may be obliged to correct it, apologise to the candidate and pay PLN 100,000 to public benefit organisations. The financing of the election campaign is strictly regulated and fully transparent – after the elections the State Electoral Commission accepts and approves the committees' financial statements; rejection of the approval causes the party to lose 75% of the grants and it may lose the subvention from the State Treasury.

D. Voters

218. The voters must be Polish citizens over 18 years of age – the electoral law does not provide for any requirement of residence or other restrictions on the right to vote. Voting in parliamentary, presidential and local self-government elections is universal and direct. Voter turnout in Poland is moderate – from about 20% in the elections to the European Parliament (2004 and 2009) to over 50% – in the parliamentary elections (as much as 61% in 2019) and almost 70% in the presidential election (2020).

219. The Polish electoral system provides for a number of instruments which are considered in the legal science to boost and guarantee participation in elections. The most important of these include:

(1) drawing up registers and lists of persons entitled to vote available to the public – any voter who finds them to be incorrect may lodge a complaint with the body responsible for keeping the list;
(2) the possibility of being added to the electoral register, as well as the possibility of voting on the basis of a certificate of eligibility to vote in a different place to that where the electoral register was compiled;
(3) alternative voting methods, especially the possibility of postal voting and voting by proxy;
(4) creation of polling stations in convenient and permanent places, as well as organisation of such outside the country, in places where the Polish diaspora is numerous – organised by Polish diplomatic services;
(5) traditionally, the organisation of elections on a non-working day (Sunday) is also considered a guarantee of the widest possible access – this is guaranteed by Article 98(2) of the Constitution.

E. Validity of Election: Judicial Model of Control

220. Polish electoral law consistently adopts a judicial model for monitoring the validity of elections and as far as elections to the Sejm and the Senate are considered, validity is determined by the SC.

221. Every voter has the right to lodge an objection to the SC against the validity of parliamentary elections (the same goes for presidential election, while the district court considers complaints regarding local self-government elections). The grounds for such protests may include a violation of the provisions of the Electoral Code, affecting the outcome of the election, or committing a crime against the election. The SC (currently the Extraordinary Control and Public Affairs Chamber of the SC established in 2017) reviews the objections and decides on them by way of a decision. Subsequently, the same Chamber of the SC decides on the validity of the election in the form of a resolution based on the report on the course of the election submitted by the State Electoral Commission and the opinion on the election objections; this decision must be made within ninety days from the date of the voting. If the SC declares the entire elections or election only of a particular Deputy or Senator invalid, it nullifies the elections and orders the repetition of the procedure (nationwide or in a given constituency respectively or orders to rerun certain electoral acts or orders which were considered as invalid. The determination of the validity of the presidential election is similar, although the SC must decide on its validity within thirty days of the announcement of the final result.

§2. Legal Status of Members of Parliament

I. Mandate of the Member of Parliament

A. Representative Character of a Mandate

222. The parliamentary mandate determines the position of the Deputies (Members of the Sejm) and Senators (Members of the Senate). It is a special status, connected with the set of rights and obligations resulting from the authorisation to exercise representative power conferred on them by the voters. The key element of the mandate is that the Deputies (Senators) represent the Nation (Article 104 of the Constitution). The Constitution also stipulates that they shall not be bound by any instructions of the electorate. This means that the Polish constitutional law adopts the institution of a free and universal mandate: an MP represents the entire Nation from the moment of election, not only the electorate or constituency. Neither the voters nor anyone else, including the electoral committee or a parliamentary party or club, can impose the way the Deputies act and make decisions. Nor can a Deputy (Senator) be recalled before the end of his or her term under any circumstances. The so-called club discipline is closely linked to this issue, i.e., formulating an order for a specific vote by the authorities of a parliamentary club – sanctions imposed by the authorities of the club may be imposed for breach of deputy's discipline, but under no circumstances may they lead to the deputy being deprived of his or her mandate. Moreover, the CT stated in 2010 (Pp 1/08) that 'an MP's submission to club discipline during voting ensures the predictability of its results and enables smooth operation of the chambers of the Parliament, which is an intrinsic constitutional quality'. The bond with the will of the club's authorities is therefore not interpreted as a restriction of the freedom to exercise a mandate.

B. Duration of a Mandate

223. The term of office of a Deputy and a Senator runs from the date of the announcement of the results of the elections, although they acquire full parliamentary status when they take their oath, at the first sitting of a chamber of the Parliament. A mandate may expire before the end of a parliamentary term only for strictly defined reasons, which are:

(1) refusal to take the oath;
(2) loss of the right to vote;
(3) making a false declaration of cooperation with the security services of the Communist State (however, making a true declaration of such cooperation does not exclude from the right to stand as a candidate or to hold a mandate);
(4) waiver of mandate;
(5) taking up one of the *incompatibilitas* posts (cf. Incompatibilities) referred to in Article 103 of the Constitution.

224. The sanction in the form of the deprivation of a mandate may also be applied to an MP by the Tribunal of State (TS) when it considers that a Deputy (Senator) has violated the prohibition on performing any business activity involving any benefit derived from the property of the State Treasury or local self-government or acquiring such property (Article 107 of the Constitution).

II. Incompatibilities, Immunities and Privileges

225. The unique status of an MP is particularly evidenced by certain guarantees that he/she is unaffected by the influence and pressure of other authorities and has specific protection against possible conflicts of interest.

A. Incompatibilities

226. Incompatibilitas (incompatibility) means the prohibition of joining a parliamentary mandate by holding of other offices and positions in the State and the pursuit of activities which may give rise to a conflict of interests. Polish constitutional law distinguishes two forms of incompatibility:

(1) Formal, i.e., a ban on concurrent exercise of parliamentary mandate and other functions in the State. It is forbidden to exercise the mandate of a Deputy and a Senator simultaneously (Article 102 of the Constitution). The mandate of the Polish Parliament and the European Parliament cannot be combined either. The mandate of a Deputy may not be exercised with the function of the President of the National Bank of Poland (NBP), the President of the Supreme Audit Office (SAO), the Ombudsman, the Children's Rights Ombudsman and their respective Deputies, a member of the Monetary Policy Council, a member of the KRRiT, an ambassador, nor with employment in the Chancellery of the Sejm, the Senate Chancellery, the Chancellery of the President of the RP or with employment in government administration. However, this prohibition does not apply to members of the Council of Ministers and secretaries of state in government administration; moreover, it is a rule that most government members enjoy deputy mandates. The Constitution also prohibits judges, prosecutors, civil servants, soldiers remaining in military service, police officers and state security services from holding parliamentary seats. Other cases of prohibition to combine the parliamentary mandate with public functions are laid down in laws, in particular those regulating local self-government, which prohibit the combination of the parliamentary mandate with the function of a councillor and the functions in local self-government administration and the position of a mayor or a president;

(2) substantive, i.e., prohibition to conduct business activity with profits generated by the assets of the State Treasury or local self-government with further prohibition to purchase such assets by a Deputy (Senator). Violation of this prohibition is also treated as a constitutional tort. For such an action, a deputy or a Senator may be deprived of his or her mandate by the TS.

227. In both respects, incompatibility is intended to rule out conflict of interest and guarantee the autonomy of an MP. Formal incompatibility is also designed to ensure organisational disconnection from other authorities in the State and freedom of decision as a representative of the Nation. However, it is not implemented with consistency, especially in terms of the possibility of combining the functions of a minister and a Deputy (Senator). As a further consequence, the combination of the functions of Minister of Justice (usually being a Deputy) and Prosecutor General, the guarantee of independence of law enforcement agencies and, more broadly, the judiciary has also been weakened.

B. Immunities

228. Immunity means the exclusion of a holder of immunity from the enforcement of criminal law provisions in order to protect his or her autonomy and avoid the fear of pressure or obstruction of the exercise of mandate by other authorities. The Polish Constitutional Law doctrine includes two forms of parliamentary immunity: material immunity, including guarantees of freedom of expression (indemnity), and formal immunity – immunity from prosecution.

1. Parliamentary Freedom of Speech (Indemnity)

229. Indemnity is a material immunity that excludes the criminal accountability of an MP to a certain extent; pursuant to the Polish constitutional framework, a Deputy (Senator) shall not be held accountable for his activity performed within the scope of a Deputy's mandate during the term thereof nor after its completion (Article 105(1) of the Constitution). This provision removes criminal liability of an MP for violating the limits of freedom of expression in the first place – but, according to the view expressed in Polish legal science, it also excludes civil and administrative accountability for the acts covered by it. However, as long as the activities falling within the scope of the mandate violate the rights of third parties, a Deputy (Senator) may be held accountable, provided that the Sejm (Senate) approves of this. Therefore, although the indemnity is permanent, it can be revoked under certain circumstances, since a crime and a civil tort usually involve violation of the rights of others. Thus, if an MP's violation of the limits of freedom of expression violates someone else's personal rights, it may result in the Deputy being held liable, following the consent given by the Chamber. Indemnity thus becomes often equivalent in its outcomes to formal immunity.

2. Immunity from Prosecution

230. Formal immunity means the prohibition of being called to account for one's actions before a court without the consent of the relevant authority, i.e., a chamber of Parliament. According to Article 105(2) of the Constitution, a Deputy shall not be subjected to criminal accountability without the consent of the Sejm. This immunity is limited in time – it covers the period from the date of the announcement of election results to the date of expiry of the mandate.

231. The consent to be held criminally accountable is given by a chamber of Parliament after its own proceedings in a parliamentary committee, and the Sejm (Senate) expresses its consent by the absolute majority in the presence of at least half of the statutory number of Deputies (Senators). However, a Deputy may agree to be held criminally accountable – thus waiving immunity protection.

232. Immunity shall include the prohibition on the initiation of criminal proceedings against a Deputy, but if criminal proceedings have been initiated against a person before the date of his or her appointment as an MP, at the request of the Sejm, it shall be suspended until the expiry of the mandate. In such a case, the limitation period for criminal proceedings shall also be suspended for that period. In other words, such proceedings are carried out without any impediment as long as the Sejm (Senate) does not demand its suspension by way of a resolution – such a resolution is adopted by the majority of three-fifth votes in the presence of at least half of the statutory number of Deputies (Senators).

233. Immunity is also connected with the issue of the inviolability of an MP. A Deputy (Senator) cannot be detained or arrested without the consent of the relevant chamber except for being apprehended while committing an offence, and if their detention is necessary to ensure the proper course of proceedings. However, the arrest must be immediately notified to the Speaker of the Sejm, who in turn may order the release of the detainee.

C. Privileges

234. The status of an MP is also defined by the rights and obligations arising from the act on the exercise of the mandate of a Deputy and of a Senator and the Rules of Procedure of each chamber. A Deputy (Senator) has the right to participate in the plenary work of the chamber, as well as to participate in committees without being a member (with some limits, regarding character of committee). He/she is also entitled to submit specific parliamentary questions (interpellation), queries and questions on current affairs (*see* below §3., II., A and B) to the Government. Deputies and Senators are also entitled to obtain information and materials from government and local self-government bodies outside the Parliament, as well as to intervene in these bodies as a representative of his/her constituency.

235. MPs are provided with funds from the state budget to carry out their activities in the constituency (organisation of an MP's office). They also receive parliamentary allowances or – if they give up their previous positions hold before being MPs– salaries.

236. MPs enjoy immunity from criminal liability – however, they are accountable to the Sejm for acts which do not correspond to 'the dignity of the Deputy', for breach of the Standing Orders of each of the chamber and for failure to carry out their duties – the penalties include, *inter alia*, reduction of remuneration.

237. MPs are obliged to make their financial statements available and to keep a register of profits received during their mandate.

238. Parliamentary clubs and circles are two forms of political organisations that bring Deputies or Senators of a particular political orientation together, usually affiliated to the party that formed the electoral committee – although it is also possible for other MPs to join; Members may also leave the club. Clubs must have at least fifteen Deputies or seven Senators, while parliamentary circles are less numerous (at least three members).

§3. Powers

239. In the Polish Constitutional Law Doctrine there are three categories of the Parliament's competencies. These are: the legislative function – making laws; the scrutiny function – exercising supervision over the activities of the Government; and the formative function – appointing the bodies of the State.

I. Legislative Function: Lawmaking Power

240. Legislation is the primary function of the Parliament as the representative body of the Nation. Only the Parliament has the right to pass laws under the Polish Constitution, there is no executive right (except a special case of martial law) to create statutory instruments, and executive acts are strictly regulated in terms of both the way they are issued and their content. According to the constitutional system of sources of law, it is statute – i.e., an act of parliament – that is the basic source of law, and acts of the other bodies, primarily the executive authority, are of a subordinate nature and must be issued on the basis of statutory authorisation and for the execution of statutes (on the mode of legislative work and categories of laws, *see* Part I., Chapter 5. Legislation).

241. The Parliament's legislative powers have been reduced due to EU membership, as much of the legislative competency has been transferred to EU bodies. Following the entry into force of the Treaty of Lisbon amending the TEU and the Treaty establishing the European Community (13 December 2007) and the Additional Protocols, the national Parliament's influence on the content of EU acts was determined by proposing the implementation of the 'yellow card' or 'orange card' procedure – which means that the Sejm and the Senate may send the Presidents of the European Parliament, the Council and the Commission a reasoned opinion on whether a draft legislative act is compatible with the principle of subsidiarity, within eight weeks of forwarding it to the Parliament. As of now, the Polish Parliament has made use of this possibility on several occasions.

242. In turn, the transposition of European directives is carried out in the Polish order only by means of statutes, adopted at the request of the Council of Ministers. The adoption procedure is set out in the Act on Cooperation of the Council of Ministers with the Sejm and the Senate (2010) in matters related to Poland's membership in the EU.

243. The legislative function and the procedure of passing laws are also connected with the issue of the obligation to notify the so-called technical regulations, which, in the light of Directive 98/34/EC, requires notification to the European Commission for their effectiveness. Some doubts arise in legal practice against this background, in particular regarding the nature of the provisions which must be notified to the European Commission under Directive 98/34/EC in order to be effective. As an example, the Court of Justice decided in *Fortuna* C-213/11, 214/11 and C-217/11 cases, among others, that provisions restricting gambling could potentially be provisions containing technical standards.

II. Scrutiny Function: Supervision of and Control over the Executive

244. The scrutiny function is an exclusive competency of the Sejm; the Senate has no such power – in accordance with Article 95(2) of the Constitution, the Sejm shall exercise control over the activities of the Council of Ministers within the scope specified by the provisions of the Constitution and statutes. Although the Sejm may also exercise certain control powers over other state bodies, e.g., by directing the desiderata to the President of the SAO, voting on the KRRiT's report, the content of Article 95(2) stipulates that the control function applies primarily to the Government. Such scrutiny has a legal dimension, i.e., it concerns the correctness (legality) of the actions of the Government and its subordinate entities, as well as a political dimension, that is from the point of view of the compliance of the Government's policy with the preferences of the Sejm, or more precisely, the majority of the Sejm. It must be stressed that under the Polish political system the control function allows the opposition to impose a small degree of accountability on the Government, because the parliamentary majority from which the Council of Ministers originated can effectively block great deal of own accountability through the actions of the Sejm's authorities, voting in committees and during plenary sessions.

245. Scrutiny may take the form of instruments used individually by MPs, or the actions of the entire chamber of Parliament.

A. The Right of Interpellation

246. Means available to MPs are the principal as well as most frequently applied instruments of parliamentary supervisory power. They are diversified in Polish parliamentary law as: the above-mentioned interpellations, queries, requests for information and questions on current affairs addressed to members of the Government.

247. Interpellations and Deputies' questions are similar in nature and can be voiced by any MP. They involve matters relating to problems of state policy and concern matters of a more serious nature. The Prime Minister and the other members of the Government are obliged to respond to such questions in writing within twenty-one days. If it is unsatisfactory, the Member submitting the question may ask for additional clarification.

B. The Right to Ask Questions

248. A parliamentary club and a group of at least fifteen Deputies may also submit a request for a minister to present the so-called current information at a sitting of the Sejm. However, the Presidium of the Sejm decides whether to meet these demands, after the opinion of the Convent of Seniors (*see* Part II., Chapter 2., §4., II. The Speaker, Presidium and Convent of Seniors, Parliamentary Committees), and if the Council does not reach an agreement on the matter, the vote in the chamber is decisive. The presentation of information by a member of the Government is subject to debate.

249. The members of the Government are also obliged to provide answers concerning the current affairs requested by the Deputies at each sitting of the Sejm, whereby the choice and order of questions asked at the meeting is decided by the Presidium of the Sejm, after consultation with the Convent of Seniors (during the sitting, pursuant to the Standing Orders of the Sejm with a maximum of eleven questions being considered). Both instruments of scrutiny over the Government can therefore be largely regulated by the ruling majority, which is usually reflected in the composition of the Presidium of the Sejm – *see* further Part II., Chapter 2., §4., II. The Speaker, Presidium and Convent of Seniors, Parliamentary Committees.

C. The Right to Hold an Inquiry

250. As stipulated in Article 111 of the Constitution, the possibility of appointing an investigative committee by the Sejm 'to examine a particular matter' is a means of control of key importance. The committee is appointed only by the Sejm (without the participation of the Senate) by the absolute majority of votes, and its composition should reflect the representation of parliamentary clubs and circles according to their size. This circumstance determines that in fact the majority of the Sejm also controls the proceedings and conclusions of the committee's activities. The committee ought to be appointed in a case that is sufficiently specific to lead to conclusions relevant to committee's function of scrutiny, i.e., a request to hold specific persons accountable, with the subject matter of the examination falling within the scope of the Sejm's scrutiny function – namely relate to control over the Council of Ministers and the government administration – that is how the CT clarified its tasks in its ruling of 22 September 2006, U 4/06. Therefore, it cannot control entities which are outside the Government and are independent (e.g., the NBP), or entities which have been appointed by, e.g., the President of the RP to perform certain functions in independent bodies (the Banking Supervision Authority, for instance). The main objective of the Committee is to disclose irregularities in the activities of the Government itself and government administration.

D. Financial Supervision of Executive

251. Financial supervision concerns mainly the adoption of the state budget – that way the parliament limits and determines the State's expenditure and the Government's financial activity – with particular emphasis on the Government's exclusive right to submit a draft budget law.

252. The Government's implementation of the Budget is subject to the Sejm's supervision. The Council of Ministers must present the Sejm with a report on the implementation of the Budget together with information on the state debt within five months of the end of the fiscal year (in Poland it is the calendar year). The Sejm examines the report, also through parliamentary committees, following the departmental scope of the examination and takes note of the opinion of the SAO on it, and then adopts a resolution on granting – or refusing to grant – discharge (Article 226 of the Constitution). While granting discharge systemically means releasing the Government and its members from accountability for possible irregularities in the implementation of the Budget, failure to grant discharge does not automatically involve any consequences, nor does it mean that a procedure for legal or political accountability to members of the Government must be initiated.

E. Other Supervisory Competencies

253. Other supervisory competencies include holding the Government politically accountable by way of expressing the constructive vote of no confidence and by not expressing the vote of confidence, as well as deciding to hold ministers and other key state officials accountable before the TS – further discussed in the chapters on government and constitutional accountability (*see* Part II., Chapter 3., §4. Constitutional Accountability and Chapter 4., §4. Political Responsibility: Collective and Individual).

III. Formative Function

254. Formative competencies are mainly related to the formation of the Government. They entail granting an investiture to the Government (vote of confidence) or selecting the Government, depending on the stage of appointing the Council of Ministers. In this respect, the Sejm shares formative competencies only with the President, so the Senate does not participate in the procedure of appointing the Government. The remaining formative competencies may be exercised by the Sejm independently, e.g., when it elects members of the KRRiT; Deputies and judges to the NCJ; judges of the CT; members of the TS or members of the Monetary Policy Council. Moreover, at the President's request, the Sejm elects the President of the NBP. The Constitution and statutes also provide for a procedure for the election of certain bodies by the Sejm with the consent of the Senate; however, the lack of consent of the Senate makes it necessary to elect another person for a given position. This applies to constitutional bodies: the Ombudsman or the President of the SAO; and statutory bodies: the Ombudsman for Children.

255. The table below presents the mode of election of authorities and state administration bodies:

Position	*Elected by*	*Term of Office*	*Mode*
Members of the TS	Speaker of the Sejm or 35 Deputies	4 years (term of office of the Sejm)	Without the consent of the Senate
Judges of the CT	The Presidium of the Sejm or 50 Members	9 years (individual term)	Without the consent of the Senate
Members of the NCJ (4 members from among MPs and 15 members from among judges)	2,000 citizens, 25 judges nominate candidates, indicated by their parliamentary clubs	4 years	Without the consent of the Senate (the Senate appoints 2 members from among Senators)
Members of the National Broadcasting Council	Speaker of the Sejm or 35 Deputies	6 years	2 members are appointed by the Senate
The Ombudsman	Speaker of the Sejm or 35 Deputies	5 years	Consent of the Senate

Position	*Elected by*	*Term of Office*	*Mode*
President of the SAO	Speaker of the Sejm or 35 Deputies	6 years	Consent of the Senate
President of the NBP	President of the RP	6 years	Without the consent of the Senate
Members of the Monetary Policy Council (3)	Speaker of the Sejm or 35 Deputies	6 years	The other members are appointed by the Senate (3) and the President (3)
The Ombudsman for Children	Speaker of the Sejm or 35 Deputies, Speaker of the Senate, 15 Senators	5 years	Consent of the Senate
President of the Personal Data Protection Office	Speaker of the Sejm or 35 Deputies	4 years	Consent of the Senate
President of the Institute of National Remembrance	Board of the Institute of National Remembrance	5 years	Consent of the Senate
President of the Office of Electronic Communications	Prime Minister	5 years	Consent of the Senate

§4. The Workings of Parliament

I. Term of Office, Autonomy, Quorum and Majority

256. The organisation and functioning of the Parliament is subject to the rules of procedure of each of the chambers (as well as rules governing the National Assembly). It is an expression of the principle of the Parliament's autonomy, according to which a representative body acting as the depository of the sovereign power of the Nation cannot be bound by the will of another state body regarding its mode of operation and internal organisation (Articles 112 and 114 of the Constitution).

257. The principle of autonomy is additionally linked to the principle of discontinuation, related to the term of parliament. According to this principle, matters that remained unresolved during the previous parliamentary term (e.g., draft laws, investigations) are considered to be non-existent in the next, so that the newly elected parliament is not bound in its work by initiatives of its predecessors.

258. According to Article 98 of the Constitution, the Sejm and the Senate are elected for four-year term of office – the Senate functions concurrently with the Sejm, and the elections to both chambers are held together.

259. The term of office starts on the day of the first sitting of the newly elected Sejm and ends on the day preceding the first assembly of the Sejm elected next. The Parliament therefore works on a continuous basis, without interruption between parliamentary terms.

260. There are three situations in which parliamentary term may be shortened:

(1) The Sejm may decide to dissolve itself, by the majority of two-thirds of the votes, in the presence of half the statutory number of Deputies.
(2) The President may decide to dissolve both chambers and order new elections if, within four months of the submission of a draft budget law, it has not been adopted and presented to the President for signature; this competency shall expire fourteen days after that date.
(3) The President shall be obliged to dissolve the Parliament if the Council of Ministers is not appointed in the third, final stage of the procedure for the appointment of the Government.

261. The Polish Parliament works continuously, i.e., it does not convene for sessions, but works on a permanent basis, during sittings summoned by chamber leaders (marshals/speakers). In March 2020, the Sejm decided to amend its Standing Orders (*official title of its rules of procedure*), so that sessions can be held remotely under special circumstances. This includes voting. The Senate also adopted a similar change, and both were introduced following the COVID-19 pandemic.

262. In principle, decisions are taken in both chambers by the simple majority and the quorum is half the statutory number of MPs.

263. The absolute majority is required by, e.g., the election of certain persons for the posts to be filled by the Sejm, including the appointment of the Government.

II. The Speaker, Presidium and Convent of Seniors, Parliamentary Committees

264. The bodies of the Sejm are: the Speaker of the Sejm (*the Marshal of the Sejm*), the Presidium of the Sejm, the Convent of Seniors and the committees of the Sejm.

265. As stipulated in Article 110(2) of the Constitution, the Speaker of the Sejm shall preside over the debates of the Sejm, safeguard the rights of the Sejm as well as represent the Sejm in external matters. The Speaker is elected by the Sejm from among its members, during its first sitting and plays a key role in the organisation of the work of the Sejm; the Speaker summons sittings, prepares their agenda (after consultation with the Convent of Seniors), decides on starting of legislative initiatives, and chooses the course of proceedings involving draft laws and resolutions. Additionally, he/she is responsible for maintaining order in the chamber, especially during sittings.

266. The Sejm also elects Vice-Marshals who perform the tasks assigned to them by the Speaker of the Sejm. The number of Vice-Marshals is determined each time by a resolution of the Sejm – usually each parliamentary club has its own deputy marshal.

267. Apart from that, the Speaker of the Sejm performs a crucial political function due to the fact that he has been selected to substitute for the Head of State. The Speaker of the Senate replaces him/her in this capacity. Furthermore, the Speaker calls for presidential election and the constitutional referendum.

268. The Presidium of the Sejm specifies the agenda of the chamber's work (following the opinion of the Convent of Seniors), interprets the Sejm's standing orders and arranges cooperation between the parliamentary committees.

269. The Convent of Seniors is a consultative body; it consists of the Speaker, Vice-Marshals and chairpersons or vice-chairpersons of clubs and circles which reflected separate electoral lists on the election day. This body uses consensus in order to eliminate disputes between the clubs during plenary sessions, especially those concerning the mode of work and organisation of the Sejm. Therefore, the Convent of Seniors gives its opinion on the Sejm's draft work schedule, draft daily agenda, motions concerning the mode of discussion in the Sejm and the election of the bodies of the Sejm, as well as other matters forwarded by the Speaker or Presidium of the Sejm.

270. Sejm committees are auxiliary bodies of the chamber; they prepare matters that are the subject of the Sejm's proceedings and also express opinions on matters communicated by the Speaker or the Presidium of the Sejm. The outcome of the committees' activities takes the form of a report and is subject to a decision during the chamber's plenary session. Article 110 of the Constitution lists two types of Sejm committees: standing and special. The former are provided for in the Sejm's by-laws, and include primarily committees responsible for the scope of work of relevant government departments (e.g., national defence, education, culture and the media), as well as the legislative committee and the public finance committee. Special committees may be constituted anytime by the Sejm by way of a resolution in order to address a specific problem. Investigative committees are a separate type (*see* Part II., Chapter 2, §3., II., C. The Right to Hold an Inquiry).

§5. Senate

271. The Senate is the second chamber of the Polish Parliament, elected concurrently with the Sejm for the identical term of office.

272. By contrast, under current model of the differentiated and asymmetrical bicameralism, the Senate has been given a smaller number of functions and powers, especially in the legislative process. It has no oversight powers over the Government, nor does it participate in its formation. As for the other areas, the Senate exercises its powers independently of the Sejm (e.g., granting consent to the President's call for a referendum) or jointly with the Sejm (e.g., expressing consent to the appointment of the Ombudsman).

273. Meanwhile, the Senate also holds the power to legislate; it may propose a bill to amend the Constitution and pass it in the wording adopted by the Sejm by the absolute majority of votes; it may also propose a motion to hold a constitutional referendum.

274. As part of its legislative function, the Senate may exercise the right of legislative initiative by submitting a bill as a body. Then, as part of the legislative procedure, it may adopt the bill without changes, adopt amendments or reject it in its entirety. The fate of a resolution on amendments and rejection of a bill is decided by the Sejm.

275. Within the framework of decision-making powers in certain matters of domestic and foreign policy, the Senate gives consent to the call for a referendum made by the President of the RP and passes a statute expressing consent to ratification of an international agreement.

276. Among the formative powers one can indicate the competency to appoint own members of the KRRiT, to elect Senators to the NCJ; to appoint members of the Monetary Policy Council, to express consent to appoint the Ombudsman or the President of the SAO (*see* the table above showing the formative competencies of the Sejm).

277. The Senate, much like the Sejm, adopts its rules of procedure, which share the status with the Standing Orders of the Sejm.

278. The internal organisation and the mode of operation of the Senate are quite similar to those outlined in relation to the Sejm. The bodies of the Senate are: the Speaker of the Senate (*the Marshal of the Senate*), the Presidium of the Senate, the Convent of Seniors and committees of the Senate. The Senate deliberates openly and continuously.

§6. The Status of National Assembly

279. Both chambers of the Polish Parliament have their competencies and tasks clearly defined, usually exercised separately. Yet, there is another autonomous body consisting of both these chambers deliberating simultaneously – the National Assembly.

280. As provided for in Article 114 of the Constitution, in instances specified therein, the Sejm and the Senate, sitting in joint session, shall act as the National Assembly, with the Marshal of the Sejm presiding or, in his absence, the Marshal of the Senate. Consequently, this body meets only for the exercise of its own prerogatives, and its work does not have a permanent or session character.

281. Although the constitutional regulation is very sparse in that respect, the political nature and competencies of the National Assembly are strictly defined. It is therefore a representative body (composed of Deputies and Senators) with its own term of office (determined by the rotation of the Sejm and the Senate). The powers of the Assembly include primarily taking the oath from the newly elected President (Article 130 of the Constitution). The National Assembly also declares the President's permanent incapacity to exercise assigned duties due to health problems; such declaration shall require a resolution adopted by the majority vote of at least two-thirds of the statutory number of members of the National Assembly (i.e., at least 374 out of 560), as stipulated in Article 131(2) item 4 of the Polish Constitution. This body brings an indictment against the President before the State Tribunal (Article 145 of the Constitution). It does so by a resolution adopted by the majority of at least two-thirds of the statutory number of members of the National Assembly. The motion in this matter must be submitted by at least 140 members of this body.

282. The Speaker of the Sejm is also constitutionally obliged to convene the Assembly if the President of the RP wishes to deliver a Message to this body (Article 140 of the Constitution).

283. A distinction should be made between the institution of the National Assembly and a joint meeting of Deputies and Senators meeting under the joint chairmanship of the Speakers of the Sejm and the Senate, which may be convened at particularly important moments both for the State and for the legislature (e.g., visits by foreign leaders, particularly ceremonial anniversaries). A joint sitting is convened separately by the Speaker of the Sejm and the Speaker of the Senate, but for simultaneous deliberations held in the same place.

Chapter 3. The Executive: The President of the RP

§1. Election and the Term of Office

284. According to Article 127 of the Constitution, the President of the Republic shall be elected by the Nation, in universal, equal and direct election, conducted by secret ballot. The presidential term of office is five years, and it begins at the moment of taking oath before the National Assembly. One person may be re-elected only one more time. The election of the Head of State is ordered by the Speaker of the Sejm. Pursuant to Article 128(2) of the Constitution: the election of the President of the Republic shall be ordered by the Marshal of the Sejm to be held on a day no sooner than one-hundred days and no later than seventy-five days before expiry of the term of office of the serving President of the Republic, and in the event of the office of President of the Republic falling vacant – no later than the fourteenth day thereafter, specifying the date of the election which shall be within sixty days of the day of ordering the election. This rule may be changed only in a state of emergency, when elections, pursuant to Article 234 of the Constitution, may not be held within ninety days of the end of such state.

285. In 2020 the presidential election was planned for 10 May (ordered even before the official outbreak of the COVID-19 pandemic in Poland). Due to the COVID-19 pandemic there was no real possibility to run the election on the fixed date and there was no legal possibility to change the date without introducing a state of emergency – this situation aroused serious controversy. Eventually, the State Electoral Commission announced that it would not be possible to vote on 10 May, and the date of the election was postponed to 28 June 2020 and 12 July (second round of voting), thus before the end of the term of the President in office (6 August 2020), albeit after the expiry of the constitutional deadlines mentioned above – yet in accordance with the regulation on the vacancy of office during the term of office, applied here in analogy to the situation when the election would be considered invalid.

286. Any Polish citizen who turns 35 years of age on the election day at the latest and enjoys full electoral rights to the Sejm may be elected the President. The candidate must be nominated by at least 100,000 citizens having the right to elect to the Sejm.

287. The President is elected in line with the rule of the absolute majority of votes, which means that a candidate to be elected has to receive more than half of the valid votes. If none of the candidates obtains the required majority, new elections shall take place on the fourteenth day after the first vote. In the second round of voting, the two candidates who received the largest number of votes in the first round are subject to be elected. If either of these two candidates withdraws his consent to stand as a candidate, loses his right to vote or dies, the next candidate who received the largest number of votes in the first ballot shall be admitted to the second ballot instead. In that event, the date of repeated ballot shall be postponed for further fourteen days. The candidate that receives more votes in the second vote is elected the President. The validity of the election of the President is then confirmed by the SC.

§2. Legal Status

288. The legal status of the President of the RP in relation to the State and the Government is defined constitutionally in the separation of powers principle; the President is one of the two executive bodies. The Constitution places the President within the executive power despite the fact that he has been assigned the role of both the keystone and the guardian of the political system and the State. Additionally, the Head of State has been given the right of legislative initiative, the competency to sign statutes and to submit the suspending veto and motions to the CT.

289. The President is a key political figure balancing the other authorities, especially through the competency to make changes in the composition of the Government at the request of the Prime Minister, or the possibility to shorten the term of the Sejm (and automatically the Senate) in situations specified in the Constitution. As regards the function of the judiciary, the President appoints judges – to common and administrative courts, as well as CT. He has the right of grace (although this competency is associated with that of the President rather traditionally).

290. According to Article 126(1) of the Constitution, the President of the RP shall be the supreme representative of the RP and the guarantor of the continuity of state authority. Literally, this post is not treated as a representative of the Nation – but the State. Considering this field of presidential power, the President is assigned the representative in internal and foreign relations; guarantor of the continuity of state authority; guarantor of observance of the Constitution; guarantor of the sovereignty, security and inviolability and indivisibility of the state territory. The Constitution and statutes assign appropriate competencies to the Head of State under the above functions.

291. The Constitution provides for strict incompatibility between the office of President and holding other functions. Indeed, the President cannot hold any other office nor perform any public function, except those related to the office held.

292. The Constitution also provides for the replacement of the Head of State in the event of temporary or permanent impediment. In the first case, if the President is temporarily unable to hold office (*sede plena*), it is reported to the Speaker of the Sejm, who temporarily takes over the duties of the Head of State. If the President is unable to notify the Speaker personally, then the determination of an impediment to the performance of the office shall be decided by the CT at the request of the Speaker of the Sejm. In the event of a temporary inability to hold office, the Tribunal shall entrust the Speaker of the Sejm with the temporary performance of the President's duties.

293. Permanent inability to perform assigned duties leading to leaving the office (*sede vacante*) can be caused by: death of the President; resignation from the office; invalidation of the election of the President or other reasons for not taking up the office after the election; recognition by the National Assembly of permanent inability of the President to perform the office due to health condition; the President's removal from office following a ruling of the TS. In that case the Speaker of the Sejm temporarily performs the duties of the Head of State until a new President is elected. This solution was applied in practice after President Lech Kaczyński had died in the plane crash near Smolensk in 2010.

294. In both cases, the Constitution entrusts the Speaker of the Sejm with the replacement of the President. However, if the candidate is unable to perform the presidential duties, they are taken over by the Speaker of the Senate. The person performing the duties of the President has all the powers of the Head of State with the exception of the decision to shorten the term of the Sejm. Since the Constitution does not explicitly prejudge the possibility of such a person being held constitutionally accountable, there is some legal doubt in that matter.

§3. Powers

295. The following groups of the President's competencies are identified in the study of Polish constitutional law doctrine: matters relating to the Sejm and the Senate, the Government, the judiciary, the field of state defence and security, the field of foreign affairs and certain other competencies.

296. The first competencies to be indicated among those in relation to the Sejm and the Senate include ordering the elections to the Sejm and the Senate and convening the first sitting of both chambers. The latter is connected with the obligation resulting from the standing orders of the Sejm and the Senate's rules of procedure, i.e., to appoint Senior Speakers of the Sejm and the Senate who open the first sittings, take the parliamentary oath and are responsible for organising the elections of the Speakers of the Sejm and the Senate. The President has also been assigned the competency concerning the shortening of the term of office of the Sejm in situations described in the Constitution (lack of possibility to form the Government, failure to adopt Budget in time). The shortening of the term of the Sejm is accompanied by the shortening of the term of the Senate.

297. The President also participates in the legislative process: he exercises legislative initiative, signs statutes and orders their promulgation. The President is entitled to submit the political veto suspending the law (the Sejm may re-enact the law by the majority of three-fifth votes) and the exclusive right to lodge a motion to the CT for preventive (*ex ante*) review of the constitutionality of a statute (including the international agreement before its ratification) before signing it (the so-called constitutional veto). Irrespective of this, the President may apply to the CT for a repressive (*ex post*) review of the constitutionality of a statute on an equal footing with the other parties entitled thereto. The Head of State can deliver a message to the Sejm, the Senate or the National Assembly. The message shall not be subject to debate. The next competency in this group is to order a national referendum upon the approval of the Senate. This stays in competition with the Sejm, which has its own competency to order a national referendum (Article 125 of the Constitution).

298. Within the scope of the Head of State's competency towards the Government, the President participates in the appointment of the Government and introduces changes to its composition, as well as accepts the resignation of the Prime Minister. The Constitution does not provide for so-called presidential ministries (i.e., ministers appointed in agreement with the President, e.g., the Minister of National Defence, Internal Affairs and Foreign Affairs), as was the case in the Small Constitution of 1992). As a result, the President has little influence on the staffing of ministries in the Government. Legally, there is also little influence on the appointment of the Prime Minister, and it usually follows the will of the elected parliamentary majority. However, the instrument in the form of the capacity to shorten the term of the Sejm in the event of failure of the mission to formulate the Government may be a factor influencing filling governmental positions, including the Prime Minister. The President may request that members of the Council of Ministers be held constitutionally accountable. He convenes the Cabinet Council, which is formed by the Government chaired by the President. This entity, however, does not have the authority of the Government; it should work towards a common standpoint of both executive bodies.

299. With regard to the judiciary, the Constitution gives the President formative competencies related to the appointment of judges, the First President of the SC, the President of the SAC, the President and Vice-President of the CT and the appointment of one member of the National Judicial Council. The President holds the right to grace. With regard to the Tribunals, it should be pointed out that it is possible to refer to the CT in order to review the constitutionality of a statute and to request that ministers be held accountable before the TS (constitutional accountability).

300. In the field of state defence and security, the President's competencies are primarily related to the position of the Supreme Commander of the Armed Forces of the RP. During peacetime, the President exercises authority through the Minister of National Defence. Therefore, this function is essentially symbolic and the Head of State has no actual commanding powers. On the other hand, the President appoints the Chief of the General Staff and commanders of the Armed Forces. The military ranks defined in the statutes (first officer's rank and general ranks) are granted at the request of the Minister of National Defence. During war, the President appoints the Commander-in-Chief of the Armed Forces upon the motion lodged by the Prime Minister. Additionally, in the event of an immediate, external threat to the State, the President, also at the request of the Prime Minister, orders the general or partial mobilisation and use of the Armed Forces to defend the RP. This group also includes the competencies concerning states of exception and the state of war. It should be emphasised, however, that these are shared with the Government and the Sejm. On a different note, it is also important to mention that the state of war is not classified as a state of exception. As a rule, the Sejm decides on the state of war and the conclusion of peace. If, however, the Sejm cannot convene, it becomes the responsibility of the President.

301. As far as the sphere of foreign affairs is concerned, the Constitution vests the Head of State with the classic competency to ratify and denounce international agreements; to appoint and dismiss authorised representatives of the RP in other States and to international organisations and to accept letters of authentication and dismissal of diplomatic representatives of other States and international organisations accredited to him. In the context of foreign policy, the President cooperates with the Prime Minister and a relevant minister. At this point, it is worth mentioning the competency conflict that occurred in 2008 between the Prime Minister and the President in terms of representing Poland in the European Council. In its decision of 20 May 2009 (Kpt 1/08), the CT indicated that in this respect the bodies in dispute are obliged to cooperate and although representation in the European Council is in principle part of the internal affairs of state policy, certain issues (e.g., security or sovereignty) speak for an increased role of the Head of State. In any case, the President may independently decide to participate in the works of a relevant body, given that he/she is the supreme representative of the State.

302. The remaining competencies of the President include: the right to submit a bill on amending the Constitution; appointing members of the Monetary Policy Council as well as the KRRiT; putting forward a motion to appoint the President of the NBP; granting Polish citizenship and consent to renounce Polish citizenship; issuing orders and distinctions.

I. Countersignature of Prime Minister

303. The President, exercising his constitutional and statutory powers, issues authentic acts. In order to become valid, they require the signature of the Prime Minister, who becomes accountable before the Sejm at the moment of signing the act (countersignature). Only the Prime Minister (not ministers) holds the right to sign the acts issued by the President, which strengthens PM's position both in Government and in relation with the President. In view of the constitutionally closed catalogue of personal prerogatives, it is necessary to countersign all acts of the Head of State not mentioned in Article 144(3) of the Constitution. It is necessary to countersign all other acts. The countersigning applies only to written acts. The Polish political system does not provide for a countersignature of presence. The countersignature is associated primarily with the delegation of political responsibility, but it also delineates the scope of cooperation between the Government and the President and means the acknowledgement of the President's acts and their implementation by the Government.

II. Prerogatives

304. The Constitution provides for a fairly rich collection of acts excluded from the countersignature, i.e., the so-called prerogatives (personal acts of the Head of State which do not involve an entity bearing political accountability before the Sejm). The most important of these include: proclaiming elections to the Sejm and to the Senate; shortening of the term of office of the Sejm in the instances specified in the Constitution; introducing legislation; proclaiming the holding of a nationwide referendum; signing or refusing to sign a bill; delivering a Message to the Sejm, to the Senate or to the National Assembly; making a referral to the CT; nominating and appointing the Prime Minister; accepting resignation of the Council of Ministers and obliging it to temporarily continue with its duties; applying to the Sejm to bring a member of the Council of Ministers to responsibility before the TS; appointing judges; appointing the First President of the SC, the President and Vice-President of the CT, the President of the SAC, the Presidents of the SC and the Vice-Presidents of the SAC; resigning from the office of the President of the republic. The full catalogue of prerogatives is set out in Article 144(3) of the Constitution.

§4. Constitutional Accountability

I. The Basis of Accountability

305. Constitutional accountability of the President is regulated in Article 145 of the Constitution. The President may be held accountable before the TS (*see* Part II., Chapter 5., §3. The Tribunal of State) for an infringement of the Constitution or statute, or for commission of an offence. The President's criminal and constitutional accountability has been completely excluded from the jurisdiction of common courts and transferred to the TS (*privilegium fori*). The criminal accountability of the President can therefore be pursued exclusively before the TS. Bringing an indictment against the President of the Republic shall be done by resolution of the National Assembly passed by the majority of at least two-thirds of the statutory number of members of the National Assembly, on the motion of at least 140 members of the Assembly. Thus, we consider here the political stage of deciding whether to hold the President constitutionally and criminally accountable. When the resolution on the indictment of the President is adopted, the holding of this office becomes suspended. The responsibilities of the President are temporarily assumed by the Speaker of the Sejm.

306. The President is not held politically accountable before the Parliament (Sejm). This responsibility is delegated to the Prime Minister, and consequently to the entire government, through the institution of countersignature.

II. Proceedings

307. To find out more on the proceedings regarding the constitutional accountability of the President – *see* Part II., Chapter 3., §4. Constitutional Accountability. It should be noted that the constitutional accountability of the President has never been initiated in Poland.

Chapter 4. The Executive: The Council of Ministers

308. The Council of Ministers (the Government) is the second executive body in Poland, operating alongside the President. It is the Council of Ministers that is in charge of conducting internal and foreign policy. Its political status fits in with the functioning of the bodies in the parliamentary system – both in terms of competency and accountability before the Parliament. There is no distinction between the Government and the Council of Ministers in Poland.

§1. Constitutional Status of the Council of Ministers

I. Forming a Government

309. The Council of Ministers is appointed in the procedure consisting of three stages; the failure of a given stage of government formation triggers another. In accordance with Article 154 of the Constitution, the President first nominates the Prime Minister, who proposes the composition of the Council of Ministers. In this respect, the President is not bound by any constitutional provision and may designate any person, but it is obvious in the parliamentary system that such a decision is going to be guided by the opinion of the parliamentary majority, which will elect an efficiently functioning government. There is no custom in Poland to appoint the leader of the party that won the parliamentary elections to the post of the Prime Minister, although this situation does occur occasionally.

310. Having proposed the composition of the Government, the President appoints the Prime Minister together with the other members of the Government within fourteen days of the first sitting of the Sejm or acceptance of the resignation of the previous Council of Ministers and takes the oath from the ministers. Taking the oath constitutes the moment that forms a new government. Next, within fourteen days, the Prime Minister presents the Sejm with an expose on the Council of Ministers' agenda, with a motion to grant it the vote of confidence. The vote of confidence is passed by the Sejm by the absolute majority of votes in the presence of at least half of the statutory number of Deputies. This concludes the procedure of appointing the government. If the first stage of the election of the government fails, the second one starts. Subsequently, the initiative moves to Parliament – the Sejm elects the Prime Minister and the members of the proposed Council of Ministers by the absolute majority of votes in the presence of at least half the statutory number of Deputies also within fourteen days. The President appoints the Council of Ministers elected that way and takes the oath from its members. If this stage also ends with the failure to appoint the government, then the last stage of appointing the Council of Ministers is initiated. The initiative returns to the President who appoints the Prime Minister and, at his request, takes the oath from the other members of the Council of Ministers, again with two weeks available to do so. Within fourteen days of the date of the appointment of the Council of Ministers, the Sejm grants it the vote of confidence by the majority of votes in the presence of at least half of the statutory number of Deputies. In the last stage, the majority granting the vote of confidence changes from absolute to simple. If the Council of Ministers is not granted the vote of confidence by the simple majority, the President shortens the term of the Sejm (it is obligatory under the Constitution) and proclaims new elections.

311. The Polish political system also provides space for political agreements pertaining to elements of the government programme, the distribution of ministerial portfolios and other important positions in the government and central administration, as well as the manner of removing ministers if necessary. Such agreements are concluded by partners to the government coalition at the election stage. They are mainly of political importance and do not count as part of the procedure for the appointment of the government. On the other hand, the legal significance of the coalition agreements is important for the budgetary financing of political parties. These agreements introduce provisions concerning the distribution of subsidies among parties to the coalition.

312. Pursuant to Article 161 of the Constitution, the President of the Republic shall, on the application of the Prime Minister, effect changes in the composition of the Council of Ministers. It is assumed that the President is bound by the Prime Minister's proposal.

313. According to Article 162, the Prime Minister submits the resignation of the entire Council of Ministers at the first sitting of a newly elected Sejm. The elections update the will of the Nation and the majority forming the government. If the governing majority does not change as a result of the elections, a new government is appointed in its previous composition. The Prime Minister submits the resignation of the Council of Ministers also in the following instances: when the vote of confidence in the Council of Ministers has not been passed by the Sejm; when the vote of no confidence has been passed against the Council of Ministers; when the Prime Minister has resigned from the office voluntarily. In the last event, however, the President may refuse to accept the resignation. When accepting the resignation of the Council of Ministers, the President entrusts it with the further performance of its duties until a new Council of Ministers is appointed.

II. Composition and Organisation of the Government

314. According to Article 147 of the Constitution, the Council of Ministers shall be composed of the President of the Council of Ministers (the Prime Minister) and ministers. Vice-Presidents of the Council of Ministers may also be appointed within the Council of Ministers. The Constitution does not specify the number of ministers and vice-presidents in the Council of Ministers, and the President and the Vice-President of the Council of Ministers may also act as ministers. Moreover, the chairpersons of committees specified in the statutes may also be appointed to the Council of Ministers (currently there is no such entity). A member of the Council of Ministers may not carry out activities in conflict with his/her other public responsibilities (*incompatibilitas*).

315. The Prime Minister plays a special role in the Government. It is a central body enjoying autonomous status and cannot be considered merely *primus inter pares*. Its special position is evidenced principally by its competencies, which go well beyond organising and directing the work of the Government. These include: representing the Government; managing its work; issuing regulations; ensuring the implementation of the policies adopted by the Council of Ministers and defining the methods of its implementation; coordinating and controlling the work of the members of the Council of Ministers; exercising supervision over local self-government within the limits and forms laid down in the Constitution and statute. Moreover, the Prime Minister is the head of the civil service corps. What is more, only the Prime Minister (*the President of the Council of Ministers*) is authorised to countersign the acts of the President, without any participation of the ministers responsible for individual departments of administration.

316. The ministers manage specific departments of government administration (departmental ministers) or fulfil the tasks assigned to them by the Prime Minister (ministers without portfolio). A separate act regulates the departments of government administration without assigning them to individual ministers. This provides some liberty in terms of the number of positions in the Government and the scope of activity of individual ministers. The Prime Minister decides on the assignment of departments. The Constitution grants the competency to issue regulations to departmental ministers, but such regulations can only be issued when there is an explicit statutory authorisation. At the request of the Prime Minister, the Council of Ministers may repeal a regulation or order of a minister.

§2. Powers

317. The Government is formed to conduct state policy, both domestic and foreign, and to manage the government administration. The relevant literature distinguishes four basic functions of the Council of Ministers that correspond to specific competencies. First, it is a function in the field of lawmaking and its supervision (e.g., it issues regulations and resolutions; it has the right of legislative initiative; it considers its own bills to be urgent; it repeals regulations and orders of the minister at the request of the Prime Minister). Second, the executive function (it ensures the execution of laws by issuing regulations and through supervision and coordination of activities; manages the execution of the Budget and presents a report on the execution of the Budget Law). Next, there is the governance function (it ensures the internal security of the State and public order; the same goes for external security of the State; it is also responsible for general management in the field of relations with other States and international organisations; it is responsible for general management in the field of the defence of the country; sets the guidelines for state policy). The last one is the management and coordination function (it coordinates and supervises the work of government administration bodies; it performs the activities of managing and supervising voivode as a government representative in a voivodeship).

318. The Government has its own representatives throughout the country – in the voivodeship, the voivode represents the Council of Ministers. It is important to emphasise at this point that a voivode is not considered a local self-government body.

319. The rules governing the Council of Ministers also specify the organisation and work modes. In this respect, it enjoys statutory autonomy, which means that other authorities are not allowed to interfere with the content of its rules of procedure.

I. Presumption of Competencies

320. It is not easy to clearly and fully identify, classify and, most importantly, limit the predefined competencies of the executive. Pursuant to Article 146(1) of the Constitution, the Council of Ministers shall conduct the internal affairs and foreign policy of the RP, meaning that the Government shall be responsible for conducting all matters and activities related to the functioning of the State, both in domestic and international relations. The Government's task formulated as such is reinforced by the presumption of competency contained in Article 146(2), according to which the Council of Ministers shall conduct the affairs of State not reserved to other State organs or local self-government. Thus, if a category of matters falling within the scope of state policy is not explicitly assigned to another body, the Government is responsible for organising and dealing with such matters. State policy should be understood broadly here – as all matters concerning the organisation and functioning of the State.

II. Powers Regarding Parliament

321. The Council of Ministers guarantees the proper execution of statutes. In order to do so, the Government is given the power to issue regulations – they can be issued either by the Prime Minister, individual ministers (only departmental) or the entire Council of Ministers.

322. In addition, the Council of Ministers has the right of legislative initiative, which entails special responsibilities regarding the preparation of bills, the right to grant them the urgency clause, that is, to prioritise them in the course of work in the Parliament, as well as to propose amendments to all kinds of bills. Furthermore, the Government has exclusive competency to submit a draft budget (*see* Part I., Chapter 5., §2. Legislative Procedure).

323. It is the exceptional responsibility of the Government to execute the Budget – it submits an annual report on the execution of the Budget to the SAO and to the Sejm under the procedure, objective of which is to grant discharge (*see* Part I., Chapter 2., §3., D. Financial Supervision of Executive).

III. Powers Regarding the Judiciary

324. The Constitution does not equip the Council of Ministers with any instruments to influence the judiciary, although the Minister of Justice, who is a member of the Government, holds significant powers in this respect.

325. First of all, the Minister of Justice carries out the function of the General Prosecutor (with the exception of the period 2010–2016, when these functions were separated), which makes him the head of a strictly hierarchical structure of the law enforcement agency, which plays a key role when it comes to serious crimes and overseeing police activities.

326. At the same time, the Minister of Justice exercises administrative supervision over activities of courts. The power at his disposal in this respect has been significantly extended in recent years (2015–2020) – he has the right to appoint presidents and vice-presidents of courts, who are consequently answerable to the Minister in terms of managing the administrative activities of the court. The Minister is also authorised to appoint a person acting as a court director without carrying out a competition procedure and without the participation of the court president, he has the right to indicate candidates from among the judges of common courts to be delegated to other courts as well as the right to revoke them.

327. Combining the function of the Minister with the function of the head of the prosecutor's office with its far-reaching supervisory powers raises serious doubts in Polish legal doctrine – it is also the subject of criticism formulated by international bodies in relation to changes in legislation which have been introduced gradually since 2015.

IV. Regulatory Powers

328. The Council of Ministers holds regulatory powers.

329. The legal acts issued by the Government are of dual nature. First of all, they may be regulations, i.e., secondary legislation of a universally binding nature. They can be issued by: the Council of Ministers acting as a whole, i.e., a collegiate body, the Prime Minister and the ministers (departmental).

330. Regulations issued by the Government or its members constitute the vast majority of such acts in Polish legal practice and supplement the contents of statutes – in line with the model provided for in Article 92 of the Constitution, as they may be issued only under the detailed authorisation contained in the statute and for the purpose of its implementation.

331. Second, the Council of Ministers and its members issue acts of internal law, including both types of acts listed in Article 93 of the Constitution, i.e., resolutions of the Council of Ministers and orders of ministers and the Prime Minister. In contrast to the regulations, these acts are not universally binding – which means that only the units that are organisationally subordinate to the Government or ministers – i.e., the government administration – are bound by them. Orders may be issued only on the basis of statute, whereas the nature of resolutions is disputable – it is assumed, however, that they may be independent documents.

332. Acts of internal law cannot constitute the basis for decisions against citizens, legal persons and other entities. However, they are subject to scrutiny as to their compliance with other universally binding sources of law – as they are acts issued by central public authorities, and thus are indicated as the subject of scrutiny by the CT.

333. Both types of legal acts issued by the Government can also be controlled in the process of administration of justice by the courts – these are only bound by the Constitution and by statutes (Article 178 of the Constitution).

334. It should be added that the right to introduce legislation concerning the Budget, an interim budget, amendments to the Budget, a statute on the contracting of public debt, as well as a statute granting financial guarantees by the State, shall belong exclusively to the Council of Ministers (Article 221).

V. Other Powers

335. The task of the Council of Ministers is to maintain the external and internal security of the country and public order. It also generally manages relations with other countries and international organisations, negotiating and concluding international agreements, in particular, with the power to denounce them.

§3. Constitutional Accountability of Ministers

336. The constitutional accountability of ministers is of individual character. Ministers shall be held accountable for violations of the Constitution or laws, as well as for offences committed in connection with their position. Where offences are committed in connection with the position held, it is necessary that the request for prosecution should cover both constitutional and criminal liability collectively. It should be put to a joint vote, otherwise the criminal liability ought to be pursued before a common court, as it is competent to consider common crimes committed even by the members of the Government. The authority deciding on the constitutional accountability of ministers is the TS.

337. The Sejm adopts a resolution to hold a member of the Council of Ministers accountable before the TS at the request of the President of the Republic or at least 115 Deputies by the three-fifth majority of the statutory number of Deputies.

338. A view on the accessory nature of the TS ruling on the criminal liability of a member of the Government has been formulated in the Polish doctrine. The competency of common courts in this respect has not been limited, so criminal liability for such offences may be sought before them if it is not done before the TS.

§4. Political Responsibility: Collective and Individual

339. The Council of Ministers is politically responsible. Political responsibility is exercised exclusively by the Sejm. The Senate has no competency in this respect. It may take the form of joint and several liability for the activities of the entire government and individual ministers for matters falling within their competency or entrusted to them by the Prime Minister.

340. The Constitution of 1997 introduced the institution of the constructive vote of no confidence, which renders the parliamentary system rational, making it difficult for the opposition to dismiss the Government. Pursuant to Article 158, the Sejm shall pass a vote of no confidence in the Council of Ministers by the majority of votes of the statutory number of Deputies (i.e., by the majority of at least 231 out of 460 MPs) on a motion put forward by at least 46 Deputies and which shall specify the name of a candidate for the office of the Prime Minister. If such a resolution has been passed by the Sejm, the President shall accept the resignation of the Council of Ministers and appoint a new Prime Minister chosen by the Sejm, and, on his request, the other members of the Council of Ministers and accept their oath of office. The majority of the statutory number of Deputies must therefore agree not only on the dismissal of the current Prime Minister but also on the newly appointed person.

341. With regard to the minister, it is necessary to submit a request signed by at least 69 Deputies. The President dismisses a minister against whom the Sejm has expressed the vote of no confidence by the majority of the statutory number of MPs (i.e., by the majority of at least 231 out of 460 MPs).

342. The Constitution also provides for the instrument called the vote of confidence. The motion in this respect is submitted by the Prime Minister. It is not bound by any constitutional conditions and does not have to be linked to specific tasks, plans or bills. The vote of confidence shall be granted to the Council of Ministers by the majority of votes in the presence of at least half of the statutory number of Deputies. The simple majority is therefore sufficient. Failure to grant the vote of confidence obviously compels the Prime Minister to dismiss the Government.

Chapter 5. The Judiciary

§1. Organisation of the Judiciary

343. The courts and tribunals shall constitute a separate power and shall be independent of other branches of power (Article 173 of the Constitution). The Constitution does not define the concept of the court; it is assumed that it is a body equipped with power to administer justice, independent and separate from other bodies, composed of judges, i.e., persons with appropriate professional qualifications and equipped with the attribute of impartiality, examining cases and adjudicating in accordance with the requirements of procedures and in line with generally applicable law.

344. The tribunals include the CT and the TS; they are bodies of the judiciary with distinct functions, strictly defined by the Constitution and different from the courts.

345. The analysis of the rules governing the judiciary should begin with a statement that the solutions adopted by the legislator in the years 2015–2020 have profoundly remodelled the constitutional system in this respect without altering the provisions of the Constitution. The ruling majority in Poland does not have sufficient support to amend the Constitution, but has enough to introduce changes passing ordinary legislation. These changes concern in particular the mode of appointment of judges and the structure of the SC and the dependence of the judiciary. With the far-reaching politicisation of the CT, this results in informal changes of the Constitution despite their potential unconstitutional nature.

346. Below are the rules concerning the judicial powers that have been regulated in the currently valid Constitution of 1997 with the indication of areas where the practice now deviates from the adopted formula.

I. General Introduction

347. Moving on to the issue of judicial power in Poland, it should be stressed that the concept of judiciary is different from that of administration of justice. The judicial power is exercised by courts and tribunals (Article 10(2) of the Constitution). On the other hand, the system of administration of justice – i.e., the activities of the State carried out by independent courts, which consist in applying the provisions of the law in force to specific factual states of affairs, recognised in criminal and civil cases and in matters of administrative law – has been entrusted to the SC, common courts, administrative courts and military courts (Article 175).

348. At the same time, it has been observed that the activities of the TS, which adjudicates on the constitutional accountability and criminal liability of the highest state officials, are similar to those performed by criminal courts, while the CT performs tasks that can be qualified as supervisory activities. Prior to 2015, however, the CT was criticised for going beyond the designed role of a 'negative legislator'. The criticism related specifically to active approach of the CT towards creating law, e.g., through binding interpretation rather than repealing unconstitutional legal norms. Particular controversy surrounds interpretation contained in decisions in which the CT provided binding analysis despite the lack of constitutionally defined competency to issue an interpretation of the Constitution *in abstracto*. At present, however, the CT has significantly limited its adjudicatory activity. It shows a tendency to consider constitutionally dubious activities of the legislative and executive authorities as conforming with the Constitution.

349. When it comes to balancing mechanisms, the legislator has the competency to modify court judgments by way of a general amnesty and the President holds the right to apply an individual act of grace. Constitutional mechanisms stipulate the influence of the CT on the legislator's action in the form of scrutiny of normative acts and the TS' influence on the action of the executive bodies in the form of the ruling on constitutional accountability. The Council of Ministers' influence on judicature is limited. In principle, its competency is limited to issuing secondary legislation in the form of regulations. In terms of issuing regulations concerning the judicial authority, the President has also been assigned considerable significance. In 2017, the Minister of Justice was also given broad and almost arbitrary mandate to appoint and dismiss presidents of courts, which has strengthened his authority over them.

A. Dual Judicial Organisation: Distinguishing Between the Common and the Administrative Courts

350. The Constitution provides for a separate organisation of the general judiciary adjudicating in civil and criminal matters and the administrative judiciary deciding on the legality of administrative decisions. These structures feature separate instances classified as the highest levels of jurisdiction in the form of the SC and the SAC.

B. The SC and the SAC

351. The SC is responsible for the judicial supervision of the activities undertaken by common and military courts within the scope of adjudication. This oversight is mainly exercised by the institution of cassation appeals.

352. The First President of the SC is appointed by the President for the six-year term of office from among candidates presented by the General Assembly of SC Judges. However, legislation introduced at the end of 2017 was supposed to lead to unconstitutional shortening of the term of the President in office. A mechanism was introduced under which judges over 65 years of age were to retire. It was possible to extend the period of duty to the age of 70, which was left to the President to decide on. Such a solution would result in the First President of the SC, in office from 2014, losing her seat before the end of the constitutionally defined six-year term. Interestingly, in this case, the solution introduced by Poland was similar to that adopted in Hungary, which in turn resulted in the unfavourable decision of the European Court of Human Rights (ECHR, case *Baka v. Hungary*, 20261/12, 23 June 2016). Finally, under pressure of the CJEU position, the Polish Parliament withdrew from these controversial legal solutions.

353. Because of both the aforementioned and some other changes in judicial power, on 20 December 2017, Article 7 TEU was activated for the first time in the EU's history. The Commission's recommendation in this respect was preceded by lengthy, two-year process of dialogue between the Commission and the Polish Government. The core of the dialogue was the rule of law and its component associated with the judiciary. The objections relate primarily to the destabilisation of the position of the CT. As far as the courts are concerned, the objections concern the introduction of excessive influence exerted by the Minister of Justice (being at the same time the Prosecutor General) on judges (through the appointment and dismissal of court presidents in practically unrestricted manner). In the context of the NCJ, increase in the political influence is seen through the appointment of judges to the Council by the Sejm. These issues have triggered a reaction from the Venice Commission and the United Nations and are the subject of numerous CJEU rulings (e.g., judgment of 19 November 2019 in Joined Cases C–585/18, C–624/18 and C–625/18).

354. The SAC supervises the activities of public administration in cooperation with other administrative courts. This scrutiny also includes adjudicating on the compliance of local law acts with statues. In this respect the competency of CT to adjudicate on constitutionality and legality of these acts is excluded.

355. The President of the SAC is appointed by the President for the six-year term of office from among the candidates presented by the General Assembly of the Judges of the SAC.

C. The Courts

356. The common courts shall implement the administration of justice concerning all matters save for those statutorily reserved to other courts (Article 177 of the Constitution). Therefore, it implies competency of the common courts, with other categories of courts having cognition limited to cases explicitly indicated in the statutes. Accordingly, the common courts handle civil, family, labour law and social security, criminal and petty offence cases.

357. The Act of 27 July 2001 Law on the common courts' organisation regulates the structure, bodies, competencies of common courts and the principles of their functioning as well as administrative supervision over them. District, regional and appellate courts can be classified as the common courts.

358. The following divisions are created within the district court: civil, criminal, family and juvenile, labour, as well as the commercial division and land and mortgage register. Moreover, municipal divisions of a district court may be established as a remote division.

359. The regional court comprises the following divisions: civil, criminal, penitentiary affairs and supervision of the execution of criminal judgments, labour (labour court), and commercial (commercial court of law). In addition, the Regional Court in Warsaw includes the following divisions: the Court of Competition and Consumer Protection, a separate department for registration matters entrusted to this court under separate regulations, the Community Trade Mark and Design Court.

360. The following divisions operate in the Court of Appeal: civil, criminal, labour and social security. In addition, the Court of Appeal in Warsaw has the Lustration Court as its division.

361. The courts are created and dissolved by the Minister of Justice, following consultation with the NCJ, by way of a regulation.

362. The following entities are in charge of the courts: the district court – the president of the court and the director of the court; both the regional court and the Court of Appeal – the president of the court and the college of judges and the director of the court.

D. The Military Courts

363. The Constitution provides for a separate structure of military courts that are subordinated to the SC. They adjudicate on the offences committed by soldiers as defined in the Code of Criminal Procedure; these are primarily crimes violating the rules of the military service and against other soldiers. Their cognisance also covers the acts of civilian personnel committing crimes against the rules of service and against military property, as well as soldiers of foreign armed forces staying on the territory of the RP and members of their civilian personnel (civilian personnel), on crimes committed in connection with the performance of official duties, unless an international agreement, which the RP is a party to, provides otherwise.

364. According to the requirement of the Constitution, the military judiciary is at least two-instance: it is composed of military garrison courts (they serve as the first instance in all cases, except those transferred by law to the jurisdiction of another court), military regional courts (they review the appeals against the decisions of the garrison courts and adjudicate as the first instance in cases of crimes committed by senior officers, serious crimes and those committed by soldiers of foreign armed forces and their civilian personnel. The SC the Criminal Chamber deals with appeals against decisions of district courts and cassation appeals. The Minister of Justice supervises the organisation and administrative activities of military courts. Supervision of active military service of judges, assessors and trainees of military courts is exercised by the Minister of National Defence.

II. Constitutional and Legal Status of the Members of the Judiciary

A. *The Independence of the Judiciary*

365. Under the provisions of the Constitution, courts and tribunals constitute a separate power and are structurally separate from the legislative and the executive.

366. As previously indicated, the relationship between the judiciary and the other powers must be based on the principle of separation and the autonomy of the courts is a necessary complement to the principle of division of powers. However, Polish constitutional law has been subject to serious controversy in recent years regarding the formation of the judiciary and the scope of administrative supervision over it (*see* General Introduction, §2., IV. Separation of Powers).

B. *The Impartiality of Judges*

367. The status of judges has been regulated in a unique manner. Judges are impartial in exercising their office and bound only by the Constitution and statutes. This principle also applies to members of the TS. With regard to the CT judges, they are bound solely by the Constitution, which gives them the capacity to rule on the constitutionality of statutes and on the invalidity of a provision. Judges, including CT judges, cannot belong to a political party, trade union nor carry out public activities incompatible with the principles of independence of the courts and the impartiality of judges. They are therefore bound by the principles of 'strict apoliticality' and 'incompatibility'. However, judges may hold the position of an academic teacher.

368. An important guarantee of judges' impartiality (including judges of the CT) is their special material status. The Constitution requires that working conditions and remuneration should correspond to the dignity of judges' office and the scope of their duties. However, protection in this respect is not absolute and, in accordance with the position of CT (decision of 12 December 2012, K 1/12), in a situation where there is a need to protect budgetary balance (i.e., in a situation of economic crisis), it may become frozen, similarly to other professions. Nevertheless, judges' salaries have been set at a high level.

369. Another guarantee of judges' impartiality is their irremovability. The removal of judges from office requires a court decision; the same goes for suspension or forced relocation to another court or position. Retirement is provided for when a judge reaches the age specified in the law (60 years of age for women and 65 for men) or when a judge is prevented from holding the office due to illness or loss of strength. As a rule, a judge may not be transferred to another court or retired, unless this is due to a change in the court system or a change in the boundaries of court circuits.

370. Judges, CT judges and members of the TS have also been granted formal immunity in the form of a prohibition from being held criminally liable or imprisoned without the prior consent of the relevant court. This immunity is coupled with the privilege of inviolability, meaning that a judge cannot be arrested or detained. An exception is made for arrest while committing an offence where detention is necessary to ensure the proper course of investigation. In Poland, the institution of immunity has been established and regulated quite broadly. This raises objections because of extensive group of entities privileged compared to citizens. On the other hand, a wide scope of protection of the independence of judging, especially in the State with a history of undemocratic and strong interference of the authorities in the activities of courts, is well founded.

371. The way judges are appointed should also be seen as a guarantee of judicial impartiality. They are appointed by the President for an indefinite period of time, following a motion of the NCJ. Until 2007, it was assumed that the President could not have refused a judicial nomination, since the verification of candidates should take place in the NCJ, i.e., in the motioning body. Legal measures (appeals) were provided for candidates for the proceedings before the NCJ. No appeal measures were provided for in relation to the powers of the President to ensure that his actions could be reviewed. The Constitution does not indicate mechanisms for judicial review of presidential acts in the context of judicial appointments. The President refused the nomination in 2007 for the first time. Then, in 2016, the President refused the nomination once again. The candidates then brought a case before the Provincial Administrative Court (PAC) in Warsaw. In December 2016, the PAC rejected the candidates' complaint indicating that the President's competency to appoint a judge and to refuse to do so is a special prerogative, so it is a discretionary act that is not subject to the scrutiny of the administrative court.

372. In the context of the developments in the judiciary regarding the NCJ, it is important to mention the CJEU judgment of 19 November 2019, which indicated that there are doubts surrounding the independence of the NCJ, which in turn may translate into lack of impartiality for judges appointed at the request of a politicised NCJ. The CJEU judgment was transposed into the Polish legal order by the SC in the resolution adopted by the composition of the combined chambers: Civil, Criminal and Labour and Social Insurance Chambers of the SC, dated 23 January 2020 (BSA Act I–4110–1/20), according to which the rulings issued by judges appointed by the new NCJ are flawed by inappropriate composition, which may render them invalid (against the rulings of the Disciplinary Chamber). In its judgment of 20 April 2020 (OJ 2/20), the CT found this resolution to be inconsistent with the constitutional guarantee of the independence of judges and in breach of the regulation on presidential competency to appoint judges.

373. CT judges and TS members (with the exception of its president, who is the First President of the SC) are elected by the Sejm. Since 2015, the Sejm's impact on the selection of CT judges and judges to the NCJ has gradually increased (which affects the selection of candidates for judges). This has triggered constitutional crisis and provided grounds for triggering Article 7 of TEU.

III. Judicial Proceedings

374. The rules of conduct can be classified as constitutional and extraconstitutional. The first of them is that court proceedings are carried out in at least two stages, what means the right of an individual to appeal a decision to a higher court (Article 176(1)). Another principle is the judicial supervision exercised by the SC. It reviews appeals against decisions of the second instance courts in specific categories of cases and adopts resolutions to unify judicial practice. The principle of court uniformity means that all courts issue judgments on behalf of the RP, and their structure and basis of operation are identical throughout the country. An essential principle of operation of the justice system is also the participation of citizens (layman) in adjudication. It takes the form of participation in a bench – they are elected by commune councils, and social organisations and citizens can propose candidates. Since 2018, lay judges have been elected by the Senate for the four-year term of office in the number determined by the College of the SC; since 2018 they have also been members of the SC – they participate in the handling of extraordinary complaints and certain disciplinary cases. Another constitutional principle concerning the proceedings is openness (Article 45 of the Constitution provides for a fair and public hearing and the consideration of the case with the participation of the parties – exceptions are provided for in the procedural decisions).

375. Other procedural rules not explicitly mentioned in the Constitution stem from the right to a fair and public hearing specified in Article 45 and are regulated by procedural decisions (civil, criminal, administrative court proceedings, review of constitutionality) – at least two deserve to be mentioned. First, the principle of accusatorial procedure, according to which court proceedings can only be initiated by making an appropriate statement by an entitled entity – therefore, with a few exceptions, the court cannot act ex officio. The second is the adversarial principle, meaning that the court should remain 'passive', i.e., refraining from being involved in the process of providing evidence and argumentation by two parties. The principle of equality of arms is associated with it, i.e., the equalisation of the legal and procedural situation of both parties, so that they have an equal chance to argue, prove and appeal against decisions reached during the trial.

IV. State Liability for the Torts of Public Authorities (Article 77(1) of the Constitution)

376. The right guaranteed in Article 77(1) of the Constitution is a unique legal measure provided by the Polish Constitution. According to this provision, everyone shall have the right to compensation for any harm done to him by any action of an organ of public authority contrary to law.

377. It is a vital element of guarantees and means of protecting constitutional rights. It implies that the liability of the public authority for the damage suffered is connected not with the fault of an officer or a body within the meaning of civil law, but with illegal activity of the authority, i.e., the institution or unit which is responsible for the damage done. The term 'public authority' refers to the legislative, judicial and executive power, including all state or local self-government institutions, as well as others – provided that they perform the functions of public authority. The phrase 'illegality' means that not only a decision of the authority applying the law but also legislative activity which effectively deprives or restricts the possibility of exercising the rights arising from another legal act may be considered as such activity.

V. The National Council of the Judiciary

378. The authorities cooperate using the NCJ as a platform, which is made up of three authorities (judges, Minister of Justice, representative of the President, Deputies and Senators, Article 187). Article 10 of the Constitution fails to classify it as a judicial power. The NCJ's systemic role is to uphold the independence of the courts and the impartiality of judges, bringing it closer to the judicial authorities, that enjoy guaranteed independence. However, the nature of the NCJ has not been clearly circumscribed in the Constitution nor has it been agreed upon in the doctrine, thus allowing for the adoption of various solutions. Hence, in its ruling of 20 June 2017 (K 5/17), the CT stated that the principles of the functioning of the judiciary do not apply to the NCJ. This means, for instance, that it does not have to be a body independent from other authorities. As a result, it was considered acceptable to introduce a new legislation in 2017 that gave the Sejm the possibility (alongside the election of Deputies) to appoint judges to the Council. Such a relationship violates the Council of Europe's norms in terms of the rule of law. Consequently, following the Polish legislators' efforts to diminish the existing status of the NCJ, its membership in the European Network of Councils for the Judiciary (ENCJ) was suspended by decision of the ENCJ General Assembly of 17 September 2018.

§2. The CT and Constitutional Review

379. Another body classified as a judicial power is the CT. It is a judicial type entity (independent of other authorities, its judges are impartial). It is composed of fifteen judges, elected individually by the Sejm for nine years from among those demonstrating outstanding legal expertise. Re-election to the Tribunal is not allowed.

I. The Constitutional Review: General Remarks

380. The model of the constitutional review in Poland is judicial and centralised. As a rule, the CT is the only body entitled to decide on the constitutionality of a statute and universally binding acts, adopted by central authorities. As far as local law is concerned, ruling on the legality of such acts is entrusted to administrative courts and the SAC. The CT carries out an *ex post* (repressive) review of acts that have been promulgated and entered into force. What is important in this case is the operation of the statute in practice and the controversy it has caused. *Ex ante* (preventive) review concerns only laws before they are signed and international agreements prior to their ratification. Only the President may file a motion in this matter.

381. The Tribunal's review is essentially abstract; it relates only to norms, without reference to a specific, pending court case. A specific review related to a court case concerns only a constitutional complaint and a question of law. In such a case it is an *ex post* review, i.e., concerning regulations that have already entered into force.

II. Competencies and Proceedings

382. Article 188 of the Constitution indicates that the CT shall adjudicate regarding the following matters: the conformity of statutes and international agreements to the Constitution; the conformity of a statute with ratified international agreements whose ratification required prior consent expressed in another statute; the conformity of legal regulations issued by central state bodies (ordinances, government resolutions, orders) with the Constitution, ratified international agreements and laws. In this respect, the Tribunal adjudicates on the hierarchical conformity of normative acts. In accordance with the principle of constitutionalism, the constitutional regulation concerning the rights of the individual is primarily protected against arbitrary interference by any of the divided authorities. This role is emphasised by the competency to decide on a constitutional complaint. Through this competency, CT allowed for the possibility of reviewing the constitutionality of EU acts without repealing them (decision of 16 November 2011, SK 45/09).

383. The Tribunal also decides on questions of law forwarded by the court, as long as the answer thereto depends on the outcome of the case currently pending before this court. Here, the review concerns the constitutionality of the grounds for the court's decision in this particular case. On the other hand, court's decisions are not subject to Tribunal's scrutiny.

384. Furthermore, the CT adjudicates on the compliance of the purposes or activities of political parties with the Constitution. According to the CT's position, the ban may take place in the event of non-compliance with Article 13 of the Constitution. No political party has been outlawed under the 1997 Constitution (*see* Part II., Chapter 1., §2. Political Parties).

385. Additionally, the CT has been granted competency to settle disputes over competency between central constitutional organs of the State.

386. The Constitution provides a limited group of entities with the legitimacy to put motions to the CT. First of all, it defines the general legitimacy (pertaining to all normative acts) to review the constitutionality of the law and the activities (objectives) of political parties which can be exercised by: the President, the Speaker of the Sejm, the Speaker of the Senate, the Prime Minister, fifty Deputies, thirty Senators, the First President of the SC, the President of the SAC, General Prosecutor, the President of the Supreme Chamber of Control and the Ombudsman. The NCJ, bodies constituting local self-government units, nationwide trade union bodies and nationwide authorities of organisations of employers and professional organisations, churches and other religious associations are granted functional legitimacy. This means that these entities may submit a request as long as the normative act concerns matters falling within the scope of their activities. The NCJ can refer to the Tribunal normative acts concerning judicial independence and the impartiality of judges.

387. The legitimacy to lodge a constitutional complaint has been defined separately, too. Only a person with an individual and current interest, who has been personally affected by a ruling and whose constitutional rights, freedoms or duties are affected by the case, can lodge a constitutional complaint. No complaint can be made in the interest of another person.

388. The following entities may submit a complaint to the CT regarding a competency dispute: the President, the Speaker of the Sejm, the Speaker of the Senate, the Prime Minister, the First President of the SC, the President of the SAC and the President of the SAO. However, this possibility has not been attributed to the entities remaining in dispute.

389. The consequences of the CT ruling are described in the Constitution in detail. A normative act loses its binding force due to the Tribunal's declaration of its non-conformity with the Constitution. The Constitution empowers judgments with universally binding force and specifies the moment of their entry into force. The ruling functions *ex nunc* and is therefore applicable to future situations. Court judgments and decisions issued on the basis of a constitutionally flawed legal norm remain in force, while an individual retains the right to have them challenged in proceedings provided for in specific procedures (e.g., criminal, civil or administrative, Article 190(4) of the Constitution).

390. It also indicates that these rulings are published in the official journal in which the normative act being the subject of the decision was promulgated. The constitutionally defined features of CT rulings include the attributes relating to normative acts, which gives rise to the fact that CT's activity draws closer to lawmaking activity (negative legislator). On the other hand, it may also give rise to the temptation to actively contribute to the legal order. Additionally, the peculiar position of the Tribunal emphasises the finality of its rulings, which should be associated with the uniformity of proceedings. Therefore, we are dealing with a body of exceptional standing, able to interfere in the lawmaking process.

391. The Tribunal's ruling comes into force on the day of its promulgation in the Official Gazette. However, the court may set a different date for the termination of a normative act (*pro futuro* effect). This period may not exceed eighteen months for statutes and twelve months for other legislative acts. This is the time for the legislator to prepare new legal regulations, fully compliant with the Constitution. The Tribunal decides to use this option if repealing the act would cause negative consequences for the legal system more serious than if it was temporarily left in force. Nevertheless, since the moment of announcing the ruling, a normative act does not benefit from the presumption of constitutionality. This means that in their judicial practice the courts should take into account the fact that such an act is unconstitutional. It should also be pointed out that unconstitutional provisions upheld temporarily cannot justify lack of implementation of EU legislation (CJEU judgment in the case of *Filipiak* of 2009, C-314/08).

III. The Constitutional Complaint

392. Pursuant to Article 79 of the Constitution everyone whose constitutional freedoms or rights have been infringed the entity to lodge a complaint with the CT on the constitutional compliance of a statute or other normative act, on the basis of which a court or a public administration body has finally ruled on freedoms, rights or obligations set out in the Constitution. A complaint cannot be made regarding asylum and granting refugee status.

IV. Composition of the Tribunal

393. According to Article 194 of the Constitution, the Tribunal is composed of fifteen judges. They are individually chosen by the Sejm, the term of office of the Constitutional Judge is nine years. Following a balance of power, the competency to appoint the President and Vice-President of the CT is entrusted to the President of the Republic, who makes the selection from among the candidates presented by the General Assembly of the Judges of the CT. No one may be re-elected as a CT judge. A person 'distinguished by legal expertise' may stand as a candidate to this group. Therefore, the constitutional regulation provides that the selection of constitutional judges is the sole responsibility of the Sejm – it elects the candidates by the absolute majority from among persons proposed by the Presidium of the Sejm or a group of fifty Deputies. Also, as of now (in line with the pre-constitutional Act of 1985, similarly to the Act on the Status of CT Judges of 1997 and current Act on the Status of CT Judges of 2016), a candidate for the position of a judge must meet the requirements necessary to perform the office of a judge of the SC or a judge of the SAC.

394. In Polish legal practice, the custom of public hearings of candidates for constitutional judges has not been consolidated – before being elected, they only attend a hearing before by the Parliamentary Justice and Human Rights Commission. However, the choice by the absolute majority makes this requirement a mere formality, as no cross-party consensus of political forces is needed to appoint a judge.

395. The individual term of office was intended to ensure a composition of the CT that would reflect the different political forces and ensure a diversity of world views not only of the electing parliamentarians, but also of the candidates themselves – in practice, however, since the terms of office are a continuation of those that were still in place at a time when the term of office had been calculated for the entire composition of the court (until 1997) – the elections accumulate in time to allow for the elections of most of the judges by a single parliamentary composition – this happened in the 2015–2019 term.

396. The selection process in 2015, just before the end of the term of office of the Sejm, was extremely controversial – the choice of all the five judges was questioned by the President, who did not take the oath from them. The election of two of judges was deemed unconstitutional by CT. Regardless of the CT's opinion, the Sejm of the next term of office annulled the previous election and elected its own judges. This was the cause of a long and extremely severe conflict and both a political and a constitutional crisis.

397. The current composition of the Tribunal and the presence of the so-called irregular judges (i.e., the judges elected by the Sejm in place of those elected in 2015) initiated a loss of confidence in the institution itself and the judgments issued by the Tribunal. It also became the first source of the rule of law crisis in autumn 2015 (*see* General Introduction, §2., IV. Separation of Powers).

398. Constitutional judges are autonomous and impartial in the exercise of their office and subject only to the Constitution. A judge of the Tribunal is not allowed to belong to a political party, a trade union or to carry out public activities incompatible with the principles of judicial independence and the impartiality of judges. Nor may a judge of the Tribunal take up additional employment other than that of an academic, teaching or research staff member, provided that this does not hinder the performance of his duties as a judge of the Tribunal.

399. Such judges may not engage in any other occupation, whether gainful or not, which would impede the performance of duties or would prejudice the dignity of the office of judge of the Tribunal or might undermine confidence in their impartiality or independence.

400. A constitutional judge benefits from formal immunity, i.e., he/she cannot be held criminally accountable or deprived of liberty without the consent of the General Assembly of Judges of the CT.

401. Accordingly, a judge of the Tribunal cannot be arrested or detained. An exception is made for apprehension while committing a crime if such arrest is necessary to ensure the proper course of proceedings. The President of the Tribunal shall be immediately informed of the arrest of the judge of the Tribunal and may order immediate release of the detainee. A request for consent to hold a judge of the Tribunal criminally liable as well as the request for consent to imprison a judge of the Tribunal may be put forward by the Prosecutor General (private prosecutor in private prosecution cases). The consent to hold a judge of the Tribunal and to deprive him of his liberty shall be given by way of a resolution of the General Assembly, adopted by the absolute majority of votes, within one month of the date of submission of the motion.

402. Constitutional judges shall be subject to disciplinary responsibility before the CT for any breach of law (including offences), violation of the dignity of the office of a Tribunal judge, violation of the Code of Ethics of a Tribunal judge or other unethical behaviour that may undermine confidence in his impartiality.

403. At the end of the term of office, the Tribunal judge shall retire.

404. Before the end of his term of office, the mandate of a judge may expire only in the following cases:

(1) death of the judge;
(2) the judge of the Tribunal renounces his office;
(3) the judge of the Tribunal is sentenced by a final court judgment for an intentional offence prosecuted by public indictment or an intentional fiscal offence;
(4) a final disciplinary ruling on removing the judge from office.

V. The Organisation of CT

406. The bodies of the Tribunal are the General Assembly of the Judges of the Tribunal, i.e., all active judges of the Tribunal, and the President of the Tribunal.

407. Among other things, the General Assembly presents candidates for the positions of the President and Vice-Presidents of the CT, expresses its consent to the criminal liability and imprisonment of a judge of the Tribunal, declares the expiry of the mandate of a judge of the Tribunal, adopts the Tribunal's rules of procedure, and adopts the Code of Ethics for a judge of the CT.

408. The President of the Tribunal is appointed by the President of the Republic from among the candidates presented by the General Assembly – the number of candidates is not limited, the Assembly presents all the candidates who received at least five votes of support or – if none of the candidates received as many, the highest number of votes. The term of office of the President of the Tribunal lasts six years but expires earlier if the term of office of the judge appointed to this post expires. The Vice-President of the CT replaces a president in matters determined by the President of the Tribunal.

409. The President of the Tribunal manages the work of the Tribunal and represents the Tribunal outside. Moreover, the President is responsible for presenting annual information to the Sejm and the Senate on significant problems resulting from the Tribunal's activities and its jurisprudence.

410. The Polish CT is not organised into chambers.

411. There is the Chancellery of the CT and the Office of the Legal Service of the CT subordinated to the President of the Tribunal.

§3. The Tribunal of State

I. Constitutional Accountability

412. In Poland, constitutional accountability is exercised before the TS. This institution should not be considered on its own, irrespective of other institutions and systemic state mechanisms. On the one hand, it should be seen as one of the guarantees of the rule of law and the principle of legality (the obligation of public authorities to act on the basis and within the limits of the law – Article 7 of the Constitution) and the principle of a democratic state ruled by law (Article 2). On the other hand, it is an instrument of scrutiny, used to verify actions and persons exercising power in the State.

413. The Polish constitutional law doctrine distinguishes three functions of constitutional accountability. First is the preventive one, consisting of counteracting violations of the constitution and laws by 'senior state officials'. The second function is repressive influence perceived as a typically criminal law institution of retribution for an unlawful act. The last category is the compensatory function having a general social dimension involving a clear message to the public that holders of authority do not go unpunished for acts that violate the law.

414. The concept of 'constitutional accountability' can be defined as suffering negative consequences of behaviour (action and omissions) of the so-called senior state official which consists in violation of the constitution or statutes – other than criminal law. Constitutional accountability (legal, similar in nature to criminal liability) should be distinguished from political responsibility. The former concerns a violation of the law and is carried out at the initiative of Parliament before the judicial authority. Acts committed by persons held accountable are subject to legal qualification and entail legal consequences. The latter, however, consists in assessing the decisions and acts taken and the activities of the entity in view of the political direction set by Parliament. As a rule, this will be a responsibility before Parliament (or one of the chambers) based on political criteria and undertaken for political reasons.

415. The subjective scope of the constitutional accountability includes the act of a senior state official. These persons are defined in a binding and exhaustive manner in Article 198 of the 1997 Constitution and cannot therefore be extended by virtue of regulation by another normative act, even by statute. 'Senior state officials' shall be held constitutionally accountable before the TS for any violation of the Constitution or of the Act, in connection with their position or within the scope of their office: the President of the Republic, the Prime Minister and members of the Council of Ministers, the President of the NBP, the President of the SAO, members of the KRRiT, persons to whom the Prime Minister has granted powers of management over a ministry (there is no such an institution currently), and the Commander-in-Chief of the Armed Forces. Deputies and Senators shall be held constitutional accountable before the TS to the extent specified in Article 107.

416. This accountability is strictly individual in nature. It may be imposed on individual members of collegiate bodies for their own actions, not on collegiate bodies. In the objective scope, being held accountable concerns acts (constitutional tort) consisting in violation of the law in force, mainly of the highest rank (constitution and statutes, excluding criminal laws, including fiscal ones).

417. A constitutional tort is either an individual action or omission, carried out in connection with the position occupied (actions exceeding the scope of competency, undertaken without legal basis), or within the scope of office (actions within the scope of competency, but in violation of the law). Thus, these are actions committed during the performance of a function or holding an office. These include three forms of behaviour: lawmaking activities (issuing normative acts); decision-making activities (applying the law) that violate the Constitution or statutes; actual activities (e.g., using the post for one's own benefit). Liability includes culpable acts and omissions, both intentional and unintentional. In connection with the concept of 'culpability', the resolution of the full Tribunal of 10 June 1998 (TS ZP–1/98) is relevant, according to which violation of the law may be both intentional and unintentional; the latter occurs when the offender, without intent to violate the Constitution or the law, has committed offence as a result of failure to observe the prudence required in the circumstances, even though he anticipated or could have anticipated the possibility of doing so if due diligence had been observed.

418. The President of the Republic is held fully and exclusively accountable before the State Tribunal; both for a constitutional tort and for every crime, even common ones. The concept of constitutional accountability of the President is understood broadly and applies to any act that violates any criminal law, including criminal fiscal law and criminal provisions contained in the laws of various institutions. Thus, one may speak about the so-called privilege of the court (*privilegium fori*); the Tribunal has exclusive jurisdiction over the criminal liability of the President. The jurisdiction of the common courts is therefore excluded. In its ruling of 21 February 2001 (P 12/00), the CT ruled on the President's accountability before the TS, stating that it is absolute, since it covers all offences committed during presidential term of office, and not only those committed in connection with the exercise of that office. The President's liability to the Tribunal is also exclusive, since for committing a crime it is only possible for him to be held accountable to the TS. This special jurisdiction of the TS in relation to the person of the President is an expression of the President's special status as the highest representative of the RP and thus the highest person in the State.

419. The President may be indicted on request issued by the National Assembly, adopted by the majority of at least two-thirds of the statutory number of members of the National Assembly (at least 374 votes) at the request of at least 140 members of the National Assembly.

420. The Polish Constitution of 1997 also provides for special regulations with respect to ministers. Pursuant to Article 156 of the Constitution, the members of the Council of Ministers shall be held accountable to the TS for an infringement of the Constitution or statutes, as well as for committing an offence (also fiscal) connected with the duties of his office. Article 147 of the Polish Constitution determines who is a member of the Government and only such persons may be held constitutionally and criminally accountable before the TS. The function performed by a member of the Government (the Prime Minister, Vice-President of the Council of Ministers, 'departmental' minister, minister 'without portfolio', chairman of a committee specified in the statute and a member of the Council of Ministers) is irrelevant here. The same principles apply to everyone. The rules of such accountability of the members of the Council of Ministers cannot be applied to other entities holding managerial positions in the government administration, but remaining outside the Government (CT decision of 8 December 1999, SK 19/99).

421. Constitutional accountability is of individual nature, whereas the Council of Ministers is a collegial body. In practice, therefore, in the case of responsibility for the operation of the entire body, it may be difficult to determine the accountability of individual members of the government. All the more so as the SC (in its ruling of 6 January 1999 (III RN 108/98)) expressed the view that the objective scope of constitutional responsibility also covers the act of a collegial body of the State consisting in the failure to fulfil constitutional or statutory obligations. In this case, the omission concerned the exercise by the Council of Ministers of their constitutional powers to issue a regulation.

422. A resolution to hold a member of the Council of Ministers accountable before the TS is adopted by the Sejm upon a motion of the President of the RP (for obvious reasons, the Constitution prejudges that this is a prerogative – and therefore a competency exercised without the need to obtain the Prime Minister's signature – Article 144(2)(13)) or at least 115 Deputies by the 3/5 majority of the statutory number of Deputies. These persons may be held criminally liable before the TS for regular or fiscal offences committed in connection with their position (partial nature of a government member's criminal liability before the TS) if, in the Sejm's resolution to hold these persons constitutionally accountable, the combined constitutional and criminal prosecution was considered purposeful (competitive nature of government member's criminal liability before the TS). In such a case, the TS accepts the case that is already pending before the court for joint consideration. Otherwise, criminal liability is exercised before a common court. The adoption of this solution is a consequence of the decision of the CT of 21 February 2001 (P 12/00), which determined the subsidiary nature of this liability. The Tribunal concluded that the liability of a government member before a common court for an offence committed in connection with his position is admissible in a situation where the Sejm has not adopted a resolution to hold him accountable before the TS.

423. The President of the NBP; the President of the SAO; members of the KRRiT; persons to whom the President of the Council of Ministers has entrusted the running of the Ministry (currently there is no such institution) and the Supreme Commander of the Armed Forces are held constitutionally accountable before the TS. The criminal liability of these persons is pursued before a common court in all cases. The right to hold these persons constitutionally accountable is vested exclusively in the Sejm. A motion in this matter may be submitted by the President (the Prime Minister's countersignature required under general rules), at least 115 Deputies or the Sejm's investigative committee. The Sejm adopts a resolution by the absolute majority of votes in the presence of at least half the statutory number of Deputies.

424. To a very limited extent, the members of Parliament may also be held accountable before the TS. According to Article 107 of the Constitution, Deputies shall not be permitted, to the extent specified by statute, to perform any business activity involving any benefit derived from the property of the State Treasury or local government or to acquire such property. This is an expression of the material significance of the *incompatibilitas* rule. This prohibition is also an exception to the constitutionally guaranteed freedom of economic activity (Article 20 of the Constitution). The action described in this way should be treated as a specific type of constitutional tort with the characteristics set out in Article 107 of the Constitution. A Deputy (Senator) may be held accountable before the TS for violating these prohibitions. A resolution in this matter is adopted by the Sejm upon the motion of the Speaker of the Sejm. The absolute majority of votes in the presence of at least half of the statutory number of Deputies is required in order to pass this resolution. The Tribunal shall rule only on the termination of a mandate.

425. With regard to the constitutional accountability of persons other than Deputies and Senators, the Tribunal shall impose the following penalties jointly or separately: loss of active and passive electoral rights; prohibition to hold managerial positions or perform functions connected with special responsibility in state bodies and social organisations; loss of all or some of the medals, distinctions and titles of honour. Penalties involving loss of rights and certain prohibitions may be imposed for a period of two to ten years. As far as the President is concerned, even if the TS finds that the acts have been committed unintentionally, it shall declare that the President is to be removed from office, and in the case of all other persons the loss of the office normally falls under the jurisdiction of the Tribunal. For acts constituting a criminal or fiscal offence, the TS shall impose penalties or measures under the general rules laid down in the relevant criminal provisions.

II. The Organisation of the TS

426. The TS is composed of its President, two Vice-Presidents and sixteen members elected by the Sejm from outside the Deputies and Senators. The members shall be elected for the duration of the term of office of the Sejm, except that the Tribunal shall retain its powers until a new composition is elected. The Vice-Presidents of the Tribunal and at least half the members of the Tribunal should have the qualifications required for the position of a judge. They need not therefore be professional judges. Under Article 199(2) of the Polish Constitution, the President of the TS is the First President of the SC.

Chapter 6. Organs of State Control and for Defence of Rights

§1. Supreme Audit Office

427. The SAO (formerly: *Supreme Chamber of Control*) is the principal body of state scrutiny. This type of supervision distinguishes SAO from other auditing structures operating within the broadly understood state apparatus. State audit differs from others in terms of its overall subject matter, its point of view, which is of general state interest rather than sectoral one, and its close links with parliamentary (political) supervision over the Council of Ministers, as well as limited functional superiority over sectoral audits.

428. The SAO cannot be subordinated to any of the three classic elements of power: it is not the legislative body, although it is connected with the Sejm and participates in the performance of the Sejm's scrutiny function. The SAO is a separate constitutional body 'suspended' between the Sejm and the rest of the Government and established to supervise the activities of both the Council of Ministers and ministers, as well as the individual organisational units that make up the government administration system, and even those that remain outside.

429. The Office is subordinate to the Sejm, which emphasises its autonomy in relation to the rest of the Government and the executive authorities. Subordination to the Sejm, however, does not mean the possibility of interfering in the audit procedure and its findings. The connection to the Sejm, on the other hand, manifests itself in the possibility of the Sejm ordering SAO audits.

430. Supervisory competencies, subjective scope of supervision and relevant criteria are regulated in the Constitution; in accordance with Article 203, The SAO shall audit the activity of the organs of government administration, the NBP, state legal persons and other State organisational units regarding the legality, economic prudence, purposefulness and diligence. This body may audit activities of the organs of local government, communal legal persons and other communal organisational units regarding the legality, economic prudence and diligence. The SAO may also perform audits regarding the legality and economic prudence of activities of other organisational units and economic subjects, to the extent to which they utilise State or communal property or resources or satisfy financial obligations to the State. Therefore, it is evident that the SAO investigates different groups of entities to different extent.

431. The audit criteria provided for in the Constitution are lawfulness, economic prudence, purposefulness and diligence.

432. Lawfulness (Articles 2 and 7 of the Constitution) aims to check whether the audited entity conducts its activities pursuant to legal regulations and within the limits of the law and in compliance with it. SAO examines whether the law is observed, determines the reasons for non-compliance with the law and presents conclusions in order to eliminate the illegal condition. Economic prudence means conducting business activity in a way that allows achieving the assumed economic effects. First of all, it entails proper management of the State's assets and of both income and expenditure as defined in the Budget. Purposefulness means relevance, usefulness in meeting needs, adequacy to the adopted assumptions of the audited activity. Diligence, on the other hand, means meticulousness, honesty, accuracy, thoroughness in achieving the goal and spending the funds.

433. The SAO holds a special power with regard to the Budget. The Office analyses the implementation of the state budget and monetary policy assumptions and presents this analysis to the Sejm. It also presents the Sejm with the opinion on granting discharge to the Council of Ministers.

434. The SAO operates under the principle of collegiality, although considerable importance is attributed to its President. The President of the SAO is appointed by the Sejm upon the consent of the Senate for a period of six years and may be reappointed only once. The President may not hold any other position, except for the position of a university professor, or perform other professional activities. It is an apolitical body, which means that he/she cannot be a member of a political party, a trade union or carry out public activities that are incompatible with the dignity of this office. The President of SAO is held constitutionally accountable to the TS under Article 198 of the Polish Constitution.

435. The President of the SAO enjoys immunity. According to Article 206 of the Constitution, the President of the SAO shall not be held criminally liable nor deprived of liberty without prior consent granted by the Sejm. The President of the SAO shall be neither detained nor arrested, except for cases when he has been apprehended in the commission of an offence and in which his detention is necessary for securing the proper course of proceedings. The Marshal of the Sejm shall be notified forthwith of such detention and may order an immediate release of the person detained.

436. The organisation and mode of operation of the SAO is set forth in the relevant statute.

§2. The Ombudsman

437. The institution of the ombudsman (in Polish also *the commissioner for human rights* (official website) or *the Commissioner for Citizens' Rights* (the Constitution)) has been functioning in the Polish constitutional law since 1987. Back then, following the wave of reforms related to façade democratisation and liberalisation of political life, the Parliament passed the Act on the Commissioner for Human Rights (CHR Act); in 1989 (along with the transition to democracy), under the amendment of the Constitution of 1952, the institution of the ombudsman was covered by the constitutional regulation.

438. As a separate body, the Ombudsman position originated in Scandinavia and corresponding positions are nowadays found in many European countries, although it takes different political positions and is endowed with different competencies. The common feature of this institution is its connection to the Parliament, or more precisely, its scrutiny function – in a way, the ombudsman constitutes its extension in the sphere of human rights protection, hence its systemic position (appointment, submission of reports before the Parliament). The Ombudsman is supposed to perform the role of an out-of-court supervisor of the implementation and protection of human rights, especially those that may be violated by the actions of state administration – the proceedings the Ombudsman initiates are usually deformalised, and submission of motions does not require meeting specific requirements either.

439. The Constitution of 1997 contains a regulation devoted to the Ombudsman in the chapter on bodies of state control and law protection. Pursuant to Article 208(1) of the Constitution, The Commissioner for Citizens' Rights shall safeguard the freedoms and rights of persons and citizens specified in the Constitution and other normative acts.

440. The Ombudsman is appointed by the Sejm, with the consent of the Senate, for a period of five years (Article 209(1)) – both chambers of Parliament must agree on the candidate; however, if the Senate does not express its position within one month from the presentation of the resolution on election by the Sejm, it is presumed to have given its consent. Candidates may be put forward by the Speaker of the Sejm or a group of thirty-five Deputies. A citizen of Poland having legal knowledge, professional experience and high authority owing to their moral qualities and social sensitivity may take the position of the Ombudsman (Article 2 of the CHR Act).

441. The Constitution devotes considerable attention to guarantees of the Ombudsman's sovereignty – the Commissioner for Citizens' Rights shall not hold any other post, except for a professorship in an institute of higher education, nor perform any other professional activities, nor belong to a political party, a trade union nor perform other public activities incompatible with the dignity of his office (Article 209).

442. The Ombudsman also enjoys formal immunity, i.e., he shall not be held criminally liable nor deprived of liberty without prior consent granted by the Sejm. Such person shall be neither detained nor arrested, except for cases when he has been apprehended in the commission of an offence and in which his detention is necessary for securing the proper course of proceedings. The Marshal of the Sejm shall be notified forthwith of any such detention and may order an immediate release of the person detained.

443. The Constitution emphasises that the Ombudsman shall be independent in his activities, independent of other State organs and shall be held accountable only to the Sejm in accordance with principles specified by statute. In principle, the statute does not provide for forms of accountability of the Ombudsman. However, it is possible to dismiss the Ombudsman before the end of his term of office for a number of reasons, including: relinquishment of his function, permanent inability to perform his duties, making an untrue lustration declaration and embezzlement of his oath. The latter premise requires that the Sejm adopt a resolution by the majority of at least three-fifth of votes in the presence of at least half of the statutory number of Deputies (the same is true in the case of a permanent inability to perform duties). The wording about the embezzlement is subject to evaluation to such extent that in fact it allows for the possibility of dismissal by a qualified majority if the Sejm considers that the Ombudsman performs his tasks in an improper manner or in a manner inconsistent with the expectations of the Parliament. It should be noted, however, that such a situation has never occurred in Polish legal practice.

444. The Ombudsman shall annually inform the Sejm and the Senate about his activities and report on the degree of respect accorded to the freedoms and rights of persons and citizens. This information is not subject to debate or vote.

445. The Ombudsman intervenes at the request of citizens, their organisations, the Children's Ombudsman, the Ombudsman for Small and Medium Enterprises or on his own initiative. A request to the Ombudsman is free of charge and does not require any special form.

446. Upon receipt of a request, the Ombudsman may: (1) take up the case, (2) simply indicate the means of action available to the applicant, (3) forward the case to a relevant authority, (4) not take up the case – notifying the applicant and the person concerned.

447. In the course of pursuing a case, the Ombudsman may independently conduct proceedings in order to seek clarification, or commission the examination of the case to competent authorities (including the prosecutor's office, state control bodies, professional control bodies or the SAO).

448. The Ombudsman has the right to examine the case in the field, to demand explanations, to present files of any case conducted by public administration bodies, as well as information on the status of the case conducted by courts, prosecutors' offices and law enforcement bodies, and to demand access to the court and prosecutor's files after the conclusion of the proceedings and the final ruling.

449. After examining the case, the Ombudsman may, *inter alia*, address the body, organisation or institution where he had determined the violation of freedom and human and civil rights; request the superior body to apply supervisory measures, as well as initiate proceedings in civil cases or take part in any proceedings already in progress (enjoying the rights available to the prosecutor), request the initiation of preparatory proceedings in cases of offences prosecuted ex officio, initiate administrative and court-administrative proceedings, as well as participate in these proceedings and file a cassation against a final judgment, on the terms and in the manner specified in separate regulations. It is also possible to request the SC to adopt a resolution aimed at clarifying legal provisions which raise doubts in practice or the application of which has resulted in discrepancies in case law.

450. The Ombudsman may also: apply to authorised entities to initiate legislation in matters relating to freedom and human rights; as well as apply to the CT or report and participate in proceedings before it.

451. The Ombudsman also functions as a visiting body for the prevention of torture and other cruel, inhuman or degrading treatment or punishment (national preventive mechanism) within the meaning of the Optional Protocol to the Convention against Torture and Other Cruel, Inhuman or Degrading Treatment or Punishment adopted by the United Nations General Assembly in New York on 18 December 2002.

§3. THE NATIONAL BROADCASTING COUNCIL

452. In its Article 213(1), the Constitution provides that The KRRiT shall safeguard the freedom of speech, the right to information as well as safeguard the public interest regarding radio broadcasting and television. Under the systemic assumption, the Council is designed to be an important institutional guarantee of freedom of speech (Article 54 of the Constitution), means of social communication (Article 14) and the right to obtain information (Article 61).

453. Doubts concerning the legal status of the National Council have been raised practically since its establishment. Initially, this body was classified as an executive authority, or even treated as a state administration body. Nowadays, however, the prevailing attitude is that it is a state authority (sui generis) that is outside the separated powers, performing tasks related to state administration in matters pertaining to radio and television broadcasting. At the same time, the Council is treated as an organ of state scrutiny and law protection, especially as regards individual rights, formed as an institution independent from other state bodies (although this is not explicitly stipulated in the Polish Constitution). It is situated somewhat between the legislative and executive authorities, while maintaining clear autonomy and detachment from the Government. In the functional aspect of the separation of powers, it can be treated as a body of executive power. From the organisational point of view, the Council should also be excluded from such an affiliation.

454. The Council is a specific body in terms of its organisation. The Council itself is a collegiate body with statutory powers. It also includes the Chairperson of the Council, sometimes treated as a separate single-person public administration body. Such a structure of the institution weakens the collegiality of the Council a little, as the Chairperson has its own competencies and has the capacity to issue administrative decisions (regarding concessions). Furthermore, the Chairperson holds executive powers in relation to the Council's resolutions, represents it externally and leads its activities.

455. The tasks of the National Council include in particular:

- developing the directions of state policy in the field of radio and television broadcasting in consultation with the Prime Minister;
- determining the conditions for broadcasters' operations;
- deciding on the issues of licences for the distribution and dissemination of programmes;
- exercising control over broadcasters' activities;
- organising surveys of the content and reception of radio and television programmes;
- determining the amount of fees for granting the licence and entry in the register;
- determining the amount of TV licence fee;
- issuing opinions on draft legislative acts and international agreements concerning radio and television broadcasting.

456. The National Council enjoys competencies of the executive nature. It may issue regulations on the basis of statutes and for the purpose of making them binding. Like other regulations, acts of the Council are normative in nature, they contain both general and abstract norms, and are included among the sources of universally applicable law – as confirmed by the CT in its decision of 9 September 2004 in relation to the licence fee regulation (K 2/03).

457. The National Council is a collegiate body and according to the law is composed of five members. They are appointed by three authorities: the Sejm and the President appoint two members each and the Senate appoint one member. The appointment of a member of the Council is the President's prerogative – however, the removal of a member is not, regardless of the reason for such an act. No need to obtain countersignature for the appointment of 'presidential' members is a manifestation of the Government's lack of influence over the KRRiT activities. In a sense, this body was created in 'opposition' to the Government. Its constitutional role is to guarantee freedom of the media. The powers of the President in relation to the KRRiT belong to the sphere of 'political arbitration'.

458. According to the constitutional regulation, members of the KRRiT are selected from among those who have outstanding knowledge and experience related to means of social communication. The term of office of the members of the Council is shared and lasts six years from the date of appointment of the last member. The Act does not allow re-election, i.e., members of the Council cannot be appointed for another full term of office.

459. The status of a member of the Council stems from the principle of independence. However, it is not a clearly formulated constitutional or statutory principle. Apoliticality is guaranteed here with the prohibition of being a member in trade unions and conducting public activity that is incompatible with the dignity of the function performed (Article 214(2) of the Constitution). Also, membership in the Council may not be combined with the exercise of the mandate of the Deputy or the Senator (Article 103(1) of the Constitution). Members of the Council are also held constitutionally accountable (Article 198(1) of the Constitution) – although there is some doubt as to the scope of this liability in the absence of individually assigned competencies. The Broadcasting Act provides for further guarantees in the form of limited grounds for dismissal of a member before the end of the term. A member of the National Council has no immunity.

460. The Chairperson of the Council and their deputies are elected from among the members of the Council and can be dismissed by them.

461. The National Council submits a report on its activities to the Sejm, the Senate and the President of the RP on the yearly basis, along with information on the main problems of radio and television broadcasting. The Sejm and the Senate adopt or reject the report on the activities of the Council for the preceding year by way of resolutions. If the Parliament rejects the report, the term of office of all members of the National Council shall expire within fourteen days, counted from the date of the last resolution. However, the expiration of the term of office shall not take place if it is not confirmed by the President of the RP within the indicated period. This act requires countersignature, which must be treated as a breach of the principle of independence from the Government. Failure to act will mean the President's consent to the further functioning of the Council in its current composition.

462. The indicated procedure is being appropriately interpreted in terms of the Council's political responsibility in the event of a negative evaluation of its operations by the formative bodies.

463. The procedure of political responsibility of the Council members was implemented in 2010. The report for 2009 was rejected by resolution of the Senate on 28 May 2010 and then by resolution of the Sejm on 10 June 2010. On 14 June 2010, the President of the RP issued a decision confirming the expiry of the term of all members of the KRRiT on 24 June 2010.

Chapter 7. The National Bank of Poland

464. In Poland, the NBP operates as the central bank. Article 227 of the Constitution defines the NBP as the central bank of the state, but does not explicitly determine its status as a state authority. The analysis of the provision may lead to the conclusion that the central bank is a constitutional entity independent of the Government in determining and implementing the state's monetary policy, but not a state authority. Instead, this status is granted to the bank's bodies (the President of the NBP, the Monetary Policy Council) indicated in the Polish Constitution. However, the position of the central state authority was granted to the NBP by the CT in its decision of 13 September 1990 (U 4/90). It is also stated that under civil law, constitutionally defined NBP bodies should have the status of bodies of a legal person. The NBP is not recognised as an administrative body, nor as a classic entrepreneur, but as a specific bank, yet it acts as a state authority, at least in a functional sense, through its bodies.

465. The autonomy of the central bank is defined as stripping the executive power of its binding force influencing the bank's decisions and depriving both the executive and the legislature of the right to intervene in the bank's ongoing policy. There are five basic features of central bank's independence in Polish Constitutional Law: prohibition of direct financing of the public sector by the bank, non-subordination to government institutions, sovereignty over exchange rate policy, personal autonomy of the members of the bank's management and board of directors and the constitutional status of the central bank.

466. In Poland, such independence is guaranteed by the Constitution. It manifests itself on a financial level, according to Article 220(2) of the Polish Constitution, the Budget shall not provide for covering a budget deficit by way of contracting credit obligations to the State's central bank. Therefore, the bank may refuse to finance undertakings of 'its government'. There is also functional autonomy, which manifests itself in performing other statutory functions of the bank independently, as well as institutional sovereignty related to the unique position of the central bank in the system of state authorities and the manner of appointing and dismissing its authorities. The NBP is controlled by the SAO.

467. Being the central bank, the NBP plays a crucial role that reflects its independence and is responsible for the following:

(a) issuing money is a right vested exclusively in this institution;
(b) formulation (within the NBP, this is done by the Monetary Policy Council, a bank's body) and implementation of the monetary policy;
(c) ensuring the value of Polish currency (Article 227(1) of the Polish Constitution).

468. In Article 227(2), the Constitution specifies the bodies of the NBP, namely: the President of the NBP, the Monetary Policy Council and the Board of the NBP.

469. The President of the NBP is appointed by the Sejm at the request of the President of Poland for a six-year term of office. No person may preside for more than two consecutive terms of office. The President is an apolitical body, i.e., he/she may not belong to a political party, a trade union or carry out public activities incompatible with the dignity of this office (Article 227(4) of the Constitution). Pursuant to Articles 103(1) and 108, the President of the NBP may not be a Deputy nor a Senator. The President of the NBP is held constitutionally accountable before the TS.

470. Another constitutional body of the NBP is the Monetary Policy Council. The Council was formed as an unbiased body, independent of other authorities and bodies. The composition of the Council is determined by three separate entities, which choose from among experts – people distinguished by their financial expertise. The Monetary Policy Council is a collegiate body and is composed of the President of the NBP and nine members appointed from among experts in finance for six years, with equal number of candidates put forward by the President of the RP, the Sejm and the Senate. The motion of the President of the RP to appoint the President of the NBP and the appointment of members of the Monetary Policy Council are the President's prerogatives and do not require countersignature of the Prime Minister.

471. The tasks of the Council include setting the monetary policy assumptions for each year and presenting them to the Sejm at the same time as the Council of Ministers submits a draft budget law. The Council also reports to the Sejm on the implementation of monetary policy assumptions within five months after the end of the financial year. The Monetary Policy Council sets the NBP interest rates; sets the rates of banks' mandatory reserve and its interest rate; determines the upper limits of liabilities resulting from loans and credits taken by the NBP from foreign financial and banking institutions; approves the NBP financial plan and the report on the bank's activities; accepts the annual financial statements of the NBP; sets the rules of open market operations; evaluates the activities of the Management Board in terms of the implementation of monetary policy assumptions.

472. The activities of the NBP are managed by the Board of NBP, which consists of the President of the NBP as the chair accompanied by six to eight members, including two NBP Vice-Presidents. Members of the Board are appointed and dismissed by the President of Poland upon motion of the President of the NBP. Their term of office is six years.

473. In the case K 26/03 (decision of 24 November 2003), the CT stated that although the Constitution does not explicitly formulate the principle of independence of the central bank of the State, the performance of the tasks entrusted to it by the Constitution requires a significant degree of its independence. In its decision of 22 September 2006, U 4/06 (concerning the so-called bank investigation committee), the CT stated that the NBP enjoys a certain level of guaranteed independence due to the fact that it has the exclusive right to issue money and determine and implement monetary policy. The NBP is also responsible for the value of money

(Article 227(1)), and the Constitution does not allow the Sejm to interfere through resolutions or other sub-statutory acts and additionally defines the limits of statutory interference. The NBP operates in the area of public finance, and its competencies have been separated from those of the Government.

474. Such definition of the position of the NBP curbs the performance of the scrutiny function by the Sejm, especially in the course of an investigation conducted by the Sejm's investigation committee against central bank bodies. However, scrutiny may be carried out using instruments specified in the Constitution: pursuant to Article 227(6) of the Constitution, the Council for Monetary Policy shall annually formulate the aims of monetary policy and present them to the Sejm; the President of the NBP is held constitutionally accountable for any constitutional tort; the NBP is also subject to scrutiny by the SAO at the request of the Sejm or its bodies (first and foremost the Sejm committees). Moreover, the NBP is obliged to cooperate with the relevant authorities in shaping and implementing the state's economic policy. The NBP provides the state authorities with the assumptions of the monetary policy and information on its implementation and the situation in the banking system, cooperates with the Minister of Finance in the development of the state's financial plans, gives opinions on draft normative acts in the field of economic policy and those concerning banks' activities, which are of significance for the entire banking system.

475. The President of the NBP may participate in the sittings of the Sejm. On behalf of the Monetary Policy Council, he/she also presents this body and the Council of Ministers with quarterly information on the balance of payments and the annual statement of international investment standing. The NBP also implements the currency policy developed by the Council of Ministers in agreement with the Monetary Policy Council.

Part III. Local Government (Decentralisation of Executive Powers)

Chapter 1. Constitutional Status of Local Government

476. Pursuant to the Constitution, all inhabitants of the basic territorial division units constitute a local self-government community by law. The constitutional idea is to perceive local self-government through a personal substrate, the local community – instead of a category of power. At the same time, the Constitution emphasises that local self-government participates in the exercise of public authority. It performs a substantial part of its public tasks pursuant to statutes on its own behalf and under its own responsibility.

477. The rule governing local self-government operations within the framework of performing public tasks is the presumption of self-government's competency in matters not reserved by the Constitution or by statutes for bodies of other public authorities.

478. The territorial self-government units have been granted legal personality, which corresponds to their independence. This independence is subject to judicial protection. The self-government has also been granted ownership and other property rights.

479. The Constitution indicates two types of tasks that can be performed by local self-government. First, there are own tasks which serve to satisfy the needs of the local community (e.g., water supply, local transport). Then, local government units may be ordered to perform other public tasks if it results from justified needs of the State (commissioned tasks, e.g., conducting elections and referendums). Any disputes arising in the area of competency between local government bodies and government administration are settled by administrative courts.

480. In order for local self-government to be able to carry out its tasks, it is necessary to ensure that its units have a share in public revenues in accordance with their respective duties. The Constitution indicates that the revenues of such units may consist of their own income (e.g., local taxes and fees, property tax) and also of funds transferred from the state budget. The Constitution safeguards the financial independence of local government units by granting them the right to decide on the amount of local taxes and charges (e.g., real estate tax). For this purpose, an act imposing such public levies is necessary. Additionally, when there are changes in the tasks and competencies of local government units, the legislator must ensure appropriate adjustment in the distribution of public income.

481. The Constitution also provides for general rules of organisation of local self-government units. These units perform their tasks through the decision-making bodies (commune council, district council, voivodeship assembly/*sejmik*) and executive ones (commune head and mayor in the commune depending on its size, commune administration, voivodeship board).

482. The charter of a given unit drawn up by its decision-making body defines the internal system of local self-government units. Considerable autonomy is introduced in regulating the organisation of the unit (e.g., the possibility of further division of the commune, for instance, into villages or housing estates, or introduction of the legislative initiative for citizens). The Constitution has not provided the territorial self-government with the authority to shape laws with the exclusion of Parliament.

483. At the territorial level, it is possible to consult decisions by way of a local referendum. It may be held in a commune, district or voivodeship. In the referendum, members of the local self-government community may decide on matters concerning that community, including the dismissal of a directly elected local self-government body (councils, assemblies, and the commune head, mayor or president of a city). This institution may be likened to a recall.

484. The Constitution also provides for supervision over local self-government. It is exercised from the point of view of legality by the Prime Minister and voivodes as well as regional chambers of auditors when financial matters are to be scrutinised. This supervision involves the possibility of interfering in local government decisions and their execution. The means of supervision that most frequently interferes with the activities of the local self-government is the dissolution of the decision-making body by the Sejm (at the motion of the Prime Minister) if this body grossly violates the Constitution or statutes.

485. Furthermore, it should be noted that the SAC and other administrative courts monitor the activities of public administration. Such supervision comprises also adjudicating on the compliance of resolutions of local government bodies and normative acts of local self-government administration bodies with the statutes. However, these statutes are not subject to the cognition of the CT.

486. The Constitution also provides for the possibility of creating other self-governments which do not have a territorial structure. These may include professional self-governments (professions of public trust, e.g., lawyers, doctors) and other types of self-government (e.g., economic).

Chapter 2. Local Elections

487. The Constitution states that the local self-government units carry out their tasks through their decision-making bodies (councils, assemblies/sejmiks) and executive bodies (head of commune, mayor, president – the name depends on the size of the commune). Elections to the decision-making bodies are general, equal, direct and are held by secret ballot. Since 2014, the right to vote for local self-government has been regulated, like all other general elections in Poland, by the Electoral Code.

488. In Poland, people elect members of commune councils (including city councils with district rights), district councils, voivodeship assemblies and, since 2002, single-person executive bodies of communes – heads, mayors and city presidents. In communes with up to 20,000 inhabitants the elections are based on the majority vote (single-mandate districts), while in larger communes they follow the proportional system with a 5% electoral threshold in line with the d'Hondt rule. Such elections are held every five years.

489. The right to vote and to stand as a candidate is granted to persons meeting the age criteria, permanently living in a commune (district, voivodeship). The right to elect (active right to vote) members to a given council is also granted to a citizen of a Member State of the EU who is not a Polish citizen and who, on the day of voting at the latest, turns 18 and permanently resides in the area of the council.

Chapter 3. Decentralised Authorities

490. The Constitution dictates that the commune is the basic unit of local self-government. For its benefit, the Constitution has reserved the presumption of jurisdiction, which means that a commune is responsible for all local self-government tasks not reserved for other units. Moreover, the introduction of autonomy at both the local and regional level is provided for by the legislator. There is no such obligation in place, but this freedom may be applied to introduce further territorial self-government units. On the other hand, the legislator introduced self-governance at the local level in the form of districts and at the regional level in the form of self-governed voivodeships.

§1. Commune (*Gmina*)

491. The commune is the most basic and also the smallest unit of territorial self-government. If it is an urban or an urban-rural commune, it is headed by the mayor of the town or both town and commune, if it is only a rural commune – the head of the commune (*wójt*) and if it is a city, the president of the city. The commune's tasks include: taking care of spatial order, real estate management, environmental and nature protection, management of communal roads, streets, bridges and traffic organisation, plumbing and water supply, sewage system, maintaining cleanliness and order, local public transport, healthcare, social assistance, including care centres and institutions, public education (primary schools), upkeep of communal libraries and other cultural institutions, markets, public order and safety of inhabitants.

§2. District (*Powiat*)

492. The district is a larger local self-government unit. Districts are divided into rural and urban districts – the latter is an urban commune, which has been granted the competencies of the district administration within its territory. A rural district includes several or more communes.

493. The district self-government performs administrative functions on its territory that are not reserved for other entities. The district is headed by the executive body – the head (starosta) elected by the district council. The district self-government does not constitute a superior nor a supervisory body in relation to the commune authorities. Districts perform public tasks of a supra-communal nature, e.g., in the fields of public education (managing and running secondary schools: comprehensive schools, vocational schools), healthcare (running hospitals) and counteracting unemployment (network of labour offices).

§3. VOIVODESHIP (*WOJEWÓDZTWO*)

494. Poland is divided into sixteen provinces called voivodeships – they share the structure and tasks of local self-government, but at the same time they are headed by voivodes who represent the government. The provincial assembly (Sejmik) and the provincial board are the two self-government bodies.

495. The basic task of the voivodeship self-government is to create conditions for the economic and social development of the region. The voivodeship carries out this task using primarily the EU funds.

496. It is responsible for voivodeship hospitals, railway infrastructure and transport, as well as for managing the largest cultural institutions in the region.

Part IV. The Freedoms, Rights and Obligations of Persons and Citizens under the Polish Constitution

Chapter 1. Polish Citizenship

§1. Constitutional Provisions Concerning Citizenship

497. In the light of the Polish law, citizenship is a legal relationship between an individual and the State. It is understood as the status acquired through the legally established feature of a human being belonging to a community within the State, from which certain rights and obligations arise. In this sense, citizenship becomes the 'right to have rights', that is, an entitlement which gives rise to others. However, regardless of the assumption made, the concept of a citizen becomes tangible only in the context of the State, since it determines the status of an individual in relation to the State rather than to other entities.

498. The rights reserved for citizens are the ones that define the relations between an individual and the State, so they primarily concern the influence on the election of authorities and access to public service. The Constitution also provided the citizens with the right to initiate legislation, obtain information on the activities of public authorities and persons performing public functions. The rights reserved for citizens also include certain social rights, i.e., the right to social security and healthcare services.

499. According to Article 34 of the Constitution, Polish citizenship shall be acquired by birth to parents being Polish citizens. Other methods of acquiring Polish citizenship shall be specified by statute, which means that the category of entities to which the rights of a citizen are assigned is in fact determined by the legislative authority, not the Constitution itself. According to the Constitution, a Polish citizen cannot lose Polish citizenship in any other way than by renouncing it.

500. The Constitution provides diplomatic protection for Polish citizens during their stay abroad. The state authorities are also obliged to provide assistance to Poles living abroad to maintain their links with the national cultural heritage (Article 6(2) of the Constitution).

501. The Constitution does not differentiate the national status among its citizens. It provides all Polish citizens belonging to national and ethnic minorities with the freedom to maintain and develop their own language, to preserve customs and traditions and to develop their own culture. National and ethnic minorities have the right to establish their own educational, cultural institutions and organisations for the protection of religious identity and to participate in resolving matters concerning their cultural identity.

§2. Aliens

502. The Constitution also grants anyone who is under the authority of the RP the opportunity to exercise the freedoms and rights provided for in the basic law. At the same time, it recognises the possibility of introducing statutory exceptions relating to foreigners.

503. Recently, more and more often, international agreements have been imposing obligations on the States Parties to extend the rights hitherto reserved for citizens to include other persons. An example of such a regulation is the matter of electoral rights of citizens of the EU countries in local self-government elections. It should also be noted that in its rulings, the European Court of Justice uses the principle of non-discrimination on the grounds of citizenship towards citizens of other Member States.

Chapter 2. Fundamental Rights and Liberties

§1. General

I. Definition

504. The Polish Constitution uses the term 'the freedoms, rights and obligations of persons and citizens', and the chapter devoted to them in the Constitution precedes all regulations concerning the State (this is Chapter II, following the regulation of systemic principles). Such placement of the regulation of rights and freedoms indicates its significance in the vision of the State and society, which the authors of the Constitution have embraced, recognising that human beings and their status are fundamental values and the principal subjects of guarantees, preceding all others. At the same time, the part devoted to the status of an individual in the State is an integral part of the Constitution, although a separate regulation in the form of the Charter of Rights was being considered and planned (*see* below III. Historical Outline) during the period of work on the Constitution. The Polish terminology concerning rights and freedoms is consistent with the one adopted by the ECHR and identical to the dominant practice of the Constitutions of European countries and provides for two categories: rights and freedoms. What draws attention, however, is the order of these categories; in the title of the chapter the Polish Constitution indicates the freedoms first and then the rights. This suggests that its framers have recognised that there is a fundamental difference between the concept of freedoms and rights. It has been traditionally recognised in Polish Constitutional Law that human freedom is an innate and inalienable value, and its essence is reduced to making decisions and implementing them. Practical feasibility of exercising freedom exists independently of the State and the law; the latter is required in order to both guarantee and limit freedom. It does not stem from statutory law, it only defines its limits, and the State must refrain from taking action in the sphere of individual freedom. The State's activity is allowed only to protect freedom from violations by other entities, mainly public authorities.

505. The right is an entitlement to benefits enumerated in a normative act; it appears when the legal norm creating this right comes into force, so it is not natural and inalienable. The rights must be based on statutory acts, and in the event of a dispute between an individual and the State, it is the individual's responsibility to demonstrate the legal basis for exercising the right in questions. The State is obliged to actively ensure the exercise and protection of these rights. The differences are therefore aptly described in the following clauses: as far as freedom is concerned, 'I am allowed to do everything except what is prohibited by law', and with regard to rights, 'I may demand what the law has provided for me'.

506. Nevertheless, there are several reasons behind the fact that these differences are being blurred and the division into freedoms and rights is nowadays largely traditional and reflects the adopted convention. There is no doubt that the philosophical origin of both freedoms and rights is identical. The Polish Constitution assumes in Article 30 that the source of both freedoms and rights is the inherent and inalienable dignity of a person. Respecting and protecting this inviolable dignity is the duty of public authorities. The same refers to the obligation of public authorities to set limitations on the exercise of constitutional freedoms and rights (Article 31(3) of the Constitution). Thus, there is no constitutional basis for assuming that the sphere of entitlement, called freedom in the Constitution, is protected and guaranteed in a different way than the matter classified terminologically as rights. Moreover, the structure of individual rights and freedoms is complex; they consist of certain elements, that is 'components' of entitlements. It is difficult to classify these unequivocally into the above categories of rights or freedoms. Now, categorising these entitlements as rights or freedoms has an editorial character, rather than aiming at explaining their essence or the scope of their operation and protection.

507. However, the Constitution does not introduce the concept of fundamental rights (freedoms) – as it is done, among others, by the Basic Law of Germany or, with regard to freedoms, by the ECHR. Nevertheless, the notion of fundamental rights and freedoms functions in the Polish legal science and is also present in the jurisprudence of the CT. Though, it is usually a phrase referring to rights that are constitutionally protected or guaranteed (as the CT decided in relation to the constitutional complaint, it serves not the protection of rights in general, but the protection of fundamental rights as defined in the Constitution – e.g., the CT's decision of 29 November 2010, SK 8/10). Therefore, following the dominant view, the concepts of fundamental and constitutional rights and freedoms are identical in Polish law.

II. Sources

508. Just like in other countries, the system of human rights protection in Poland has its foundations in both international and domestic law. The principal point of reference in the system of universal protection is the Universal Declaration of Human Rights (1948), which, although deprived of any binding force, sets out some principles, including the principle of inherent human dignity and the catalogue of protected rights.

509. In 1977 Poland ratified two fundamental UN treaties on this issue: the International Covenant on Civil and Political Rights and the International Covenant on Economic, Social and Cultural Rights, although they were not directly applicable (*see* below III. Historical Outline).

510. The single most important act of international law that directly affects the standard of human rights protection in Poland is the European Convention on Human Rights and Fundamental Freedoms (1950), ratified by Poland in 1991. The significance of the Convention for the Polish system was crucial, especially in the period prior to 1997, when the full constitutional system for the protection of rights and freedoms came into being. The Convention continues to play a major role, thanks to the system of individual complaints to the ECHR and the subsequent direct impact of the ECHR case law on the situation of persons reporting violations of human rights protected under the Convention.

511. The documents mentioned above significantly influenced the content of the Polish constitutional regulation, determining the adoption of general principles as well as the catalogue of constitutionally protected rights and freedoms – although the Polish regulation includes several particular details (*see* below IV., C. Proportionality).

512. The constitutional regulation, i.e., Chapter II of the Constitution of 1997 regulates the system of protection comprehensively, consists of parts (subchapters) regulating the general principles of the system of protection, personal, political, economic, social and cultural rights and freedoms, as well as the means of protection and duties of a human being and a citizen in Poland.

III. Historical Outline

513. The history of protection of human and civil rights in Polish Constitution dates back to the eighteenth century; the Constitution of 3 May (1791) ensured equality for the nobility as well as security and inviolability of property rights, considering them a so-called the pupil of civil liberty, and peasants in turn were guaranteed stability of lease agreements (the land did not belong to them). The tradition of this regulation was continued by the Constitution of the Duchy of Warsaw (1807), which laid down guarantees of freedom of religion (Article 2) and the abolition of slavery and equality of citizens before the law and the right to a fair trial (Article 4). The Constitution of the Kingdom of Poland (1815) also contained the regulation declaring the freedom of the press, legal protection equal for all citizens, along with guarantees concerning detention and punishment.

514. The first Constitution after Poland had regained independence, i.e., the Constitution of 17 March 1921 (the March Constitution), contained a detailed provision concerning human and civil rights, drawing on French models, with the entire chapter 'Common Duties and Rights of Citizens' devoted to this issue. The March Constitution provided for the full protection of life, freedom and property for everyone, 'without discrimination of nationality, race, language or religion' (Article 95), extending this guarantee to foreign nationals under the condition of reciprocal protection. It also secured equality before the law for all citizens and free access to public offices. The Constitution contained an extensive catalogue of rights and freedoms, guaranteeing among others the right to a fair trial, protection of property, inviolability of housing, freedom of resettlement and choice of place of residence, the right to express one's thoughts and beliefs freely, freedom of the press, secrecy of correspondence, the right of free assembly and association, freedom of conscience and religion, as well as – the right to the protection of labour (treating it as the 'main source of the Republic's wealth' – Article 102 of the Constitution), the right to free education in state and local government schools and the right to social security. The March Constitution also contained a regulation under which every citizen was guaranteed the right to be compensated for any damage caused to him/her by state, civil or military authorities, through official activities that were unlawful or incompatible with the duties of service (Article 121), stipulating at the same time that the State was to be held liable together with the guilty authorities for such damage; similar liability was borne by municipalities and other self-governing authorities and their bodies.

515. The next Polish Constitution (Constitutional Act) of 23 April 1935 (the April Constitution) did not contain a separate chapter or a full catalogue of human and civil rights and freedoms, although this did not mean that the issue of rights and freedoms was completely excluded from the constitutional regulation. The first chapter of the April Constitution, entitled 'The RP', contained guarantees to ensure that citizens could develop their personal values and freedom of conscience, speech and association (Article 5(2)); the Constitution recognised the common good as the boundary of these freedoms. It also guaranteed that the right to influence public affairs would depend on the value of the citizen's efforts and merits, but could not be limited by origin, religion, sex or nationality (Article 7). It also guaranteed the State's oversight of employment and supervision over its conditions.

516. Following the ideological assumptions of Marxism, the Polish post-war constitutional regulation was based on completely different foundations. The collectivist concept adopted by the 1952 Constitution ruled out the guarantee of the sphere of freedom and rights granted to an individual in order to fulfil his or her own specific interest, which contradicted the understanding of the sphere of individual autonomy in a way identical or similar to the catalogues established and protected in democratic States, which recognise the freedom and well-being of the individual as the paramount value. It also lacked the legal means for a citizen to assert his or her constitutionally defined rights. Instead, the 1952 Constitution introduced so-called material guarantees of rights (such as 'making printing shops, stocks of paper, public buildings and halls, means of communication, the radio and other indispensable material means available to the working people and their organisations'), which was supposed to implement, in accordance with Article 71 stating that the Polish People's Republic guarantees its citizens freedom of speech, of the press, of meetings and assemblies, of processions and demonstrations.

517. After radical political changes of 1989 and amendments to the 1952 Constitution, the constitutional provisions concerning rights and freedoms remained practically unchanged for several years; as the only serious attempt to regulate the status of an individual in the State between 1989 and 1997 was made by President Lech Wałęsa and his bill for the Charter of Rights and Freedoms, submitted to the Sejm of the first term. However, this bill was not adopted by the Parliament. The Small Constitution (the Constitutional Act of 17 October 1992 on mutual relations between the legislative and executive authorities and on local self-government) did not regulate these issues, but upheld the provisions of the 1952 Constitution dealing with this matter. This had changed when the Constitution of 1997 came into force.

IV. General Rules

A. *Inherent Dignity as a Source of Rights and Liberties*

518. Human dignity has been recognised by the Polish Constitution, as well as by the Universal Declaration of Human Rights and the UN Covenants, the Vienna Declaration of 1993 as a source of human rights. Article 30 of the Polish Constitution sees human dignity as the source of freedoms and rights of persons and citizens and defines it as an inherent and inalienable feature. Respecting and protecting it is considered a duty of public authorities.

519. The concept of human dignity has not been defined in any normative act, whether national or international. Being the source of human rights, dignity is recognised as a fundamental, inherent human characteristic, which determines the uniqueness, exceptionality and respect due to every human being, regardless of his or her other characteristics. Assigning such a quality to every human being opens the possibility to speak of the equality of all the people in terms of rights, inherent nature and the inalienability thereof, regardless of their birthplace, age, physical or legal status. Dignity is also a neutral value in terms of worldview, which allows it to be seen as a superior and universal value for all those who accept the legal order of the United Nations – such was the intention of the authors of the Universal Declaration of Human Rights and the subsequent documents referring to it. The international context and origin of the concept of dignity as a source of rights and freedoms confirms that even before the adoption of the Constitution, the CT had already identified this value, deriving it from the principle of the democratic rule of law (decisions of the CT of 27 March 1993, W 16/92, of 19 June 1992, U 6/92 and of 28 May 1997, K 26/96).

520. The adoption of the notion of dignity as a source of rights indicates their legal and natural origin – and is therefore above the Constitution and above statutory law, remaining outside the will of the legislator. Therefore, the Polish Constitution does not grant rights, but guarantees them, imposing an obligation on the state authorities to secure them. Since dignity is inviolable and inalienable as the basis of the system of human rights, as well as related to being human – everyone shares the same attribute–, it cannot be differentiated, nor can it be given lower degree of protection. The prohibition of its violation is absolute and dignity itself is free of any limitations (including the decisions of the CT of 24 February 2010, K 6/09 and of 30 September 2008, K 44/07).

B. *Freedom of the Person*

521. Freedom of the person, proclaimed in Article 31, paragraphs 1 and 2 of the Constitution, is the second of the general principles of the system of human rights and freedoms present in the Polish constitutional system. According to the simplest and most intuitive definition of the term, freedom is the right to decide about one's own conduct, in accordance with one's own will. It is a category recognised by the

Constitution of 1997 as superior and deserving to be elevated to the supra-legal rank. As with human dignity and equality, the legislator does not grant itself the power to confer human freedom, Article 31(1) merely states that 'freedom shall receive legal protection'. However, the second paragraph of Article 31 seems to approximate the content of this notion in a normative way; the Constitution states that everyone shall respect the freedoms and rights of others, which is intended to curtail the exercise of freedom, and that no one shall be compelled to do what the law does not prescribe, which means that the legislature adopts an understanding of freedom in which it means freedom to act and the prohibition of coercion in addition to the requirements of the law.

C. Proportionality

522. The principle of proportionality is expressed in general terms in Article 31(3) of the Constitution which states that any limitation upon the exercise of constitutional freedoms and rights may be imposed only by statute, and only when necessary in a democratic state for the protection of its security or public order, or to protect the natural environment, health or public morals, or the freedoms and rights of other persons. Such limitations shall not violate the essence of freedoms and rights.

523. The formula used in Article 31(3) is largely consistent with the international solutions, primarily the European Convention for the Protection of Human Rights and Fundamental Freedoms of 1950 and the International Covenant on Civil and Political Rights of 1966. However, in Poland, this principle has taken on the value of a general rule, concerning all constitutional rights and freedoms, and not – as in the case of the aforementioned acts – the limit of permissible restrictions indicated for specific rights or freedoms.

524. Restrictions concerning the exercise of rights and freedoms may be established only by way of statute, and therefore it is not allowed to restrict the sphere of constitutionally protected rights and freedoms by legal acts of lower order or without any contemporary legal grounds. The statutory regulation of a restriction should be exhaustive, and therefore the possibility to regulate such an issue in an executive regulation is restrained. The regulation on the introduction of a state of emergency can be treated as a constitutional exception.

525. Restrictions concerning the exercise of constitutional rights and freedoms may be imposed in a democratic state (and not – as stated by the European Convention – in society) only if it is necessary for the realisation of the values set out in Article 31(3). The CT clarified, even before the entry of the 1997 Constitution into force, that the 'necessity' of such a restriction must meet three conditions (CT decision of 26 April 1995, K 11/94). First, the restriction must be necessary, i.e., the constitutionally indicated values could not be protected if it was not introduced. Second, the restriction must be practical, i.e., it must effectively strive to achieve and implement the protection of these values, and finally, the restriction must be proportionate, i.e., its introduction must be justified by significant (proportional to the restriction introduced) improvement in the level of protection of the values listed in Article 31(3) of the Constitution.

526. The principle formulated in Article 31(3) of the Constitution is addressed to the legislator, and each time requires analysis of the real need to interfere in the scope of right or freedom and to apply such legal measures as will be necessary to be effective and adequate to protect the values indicated in this provision. Therefore, it also means imposing an obligation on the legislator to use the legal means that are the least onerous for the entities which have the sphere of constitutional rights and freedoms limited. Interference with this legal status must be carried out proportionally to the intended objectives, so the protection would reasonably justify the intended limitation.

527. Moreover, the extent to which interference in the sphere of rights and freedoms is permissible is the 'essence of the rights and freedoms'. The concept of the essence of rights and freedoms, which originates from German doctrine, is based on the premise that within every right and freedom we can find their core, inviolable centre, the violation of which would destroy the meaning of the entire protection of that right or freedom. In its decisions indicating the unconstitutional nature of many of the limitations introduced by statute, the CT indicated what constitutes this inviolable part of individual rights, even before the Polish Constitution of 1997 entered into force – for example, in its decision of 2 March 1994 (W 3/93), the Tribunal ruled that the introduction of preventive censorship will always compromise the essence of freedom of expression, so it remains excluded because of the need to protect this freedom. The Tribunal has also developed a general rule in its case law according to which the scope of limitations upon rights and freedoms must not have the effect of nullifying the essential elements of a subjective right, causing it to be 'hollowed out' from its actual content and to become an illusion of right' (CT decision of 11 January 1999, P 2/98, 12 January 2000, P. 11/98, 10 April 2000, K 26/00).

D. Legitimate Aims for Limitation of Exercise of Rights and Liberties

528. Any limitation upon the exercise of constitutional freedoms and rights may occur only in the event of their conflict with the goods listed in Article 31(3) of the Constitution, i.e.: protection of the State's security or public order, the natural environment, health or public morals, or the freedoms and rights of other persons.

529. The protection of security is connected with the security of a democratic state – it may not only concern the military or internal security of the State, but also, and perhaps above all, the security of life of its citizens and democratic structures.

530. The objective of public order protection means the injunction to shape the condition of the State that enables the harmonious and normal co-existence of people in society (CT decision of 12 January 1999, P 2/98, of 7 February 2001, K 27/00, of 8 October 2007, K 20/07).

531. In relation to the reasons for limiting the exercise of rights and freedoms provided for in the ECHR, the list of justified objectives is extended in the Polish Constitution to include environmental protection as a reason for limitation. This objective is being indicated together with the protection of public health and public morals.

532. The premise most frequently used in the CT jurisprudence is the protection of rights and freedoms of other persons. As has been explicitly stated in the jurisprudence and the science of law, it refers to the constitutionally guaranteed rights and freedoms. In this case, the State (public authorities) plays the role of a guarantor of the enjoyment of those rights and freedoms which could be limited or threatened by the actions of other persons acting within the framework of the exercise of their own rights. In particular, if this value is found to be a legitimate purpose of limitation, it is necessary to carry out a proportionality test of the limitations introduced, especially to weigh (balance) the constitutionally guaranteed rights and the scope of their protection.

E. Equality and Non-discrimination Clause

533. The principle of equality, expressed in Article 32 of the Constitution, requires that all legal entities with a certain important characteristic be treated in the same way, with no discrimination or favouritism against any of them. Pursuant to the wording of Article 32(1) of the Constitution, this principle concerns, first, equality before the law, i.e., equal treatment in the process of applying the law to all addressees, characterised by the same important feature, and second, equality in law, i.e., in the process of creating the law, which means that everyone has the right to shape his or her legal situation on the same terms, as long as his or her important features are the same as those of other entities having the right to do so.

534. Besides human beings, the principle of equality may also apply to other legal entities. Article 32(1) of the Constitution formulates a general principle in this respect, and its particularisation is expressed in many constitutional norms, in particular in Article 33, which guarantees women and men equal rights, defined by the legislator as equal right to education, employment and promotion, remuneration for work of equal value, social security, as well as to occupy posts, hold offices and receive public honours and decorations. The principle of equality is also explicitly referred to in the following constitutional norms: Article 25, which formulates the principle of equal rights for churches and religious organisations, Article 60, which guarantees Polish citizens an equal right of access to public service, Article 70(4) on equal access to education, as well as constitutional norms regulating the principle of equal suffrage, i.e., Article 96(2) (with respect to elections to the Sejm), Article 127(1) (election of the President) and Article 169(2) (which formulates the principle of equality in election to local self-government bodies).

535. However, clear reference to the requirement of equality in the aforementioned provisions does not mean that it is not being respected for other rights and freedoms. Equality as a guiding principle, *a metanorm*, as it is called by the CT, takes on substance precisely in the context of the analysis of specific rights, as Article 32(1) guarantees a certain standard of creation of rights and freedoms by the legislator and the standard of exercising them (CT decision of 13 January 2004, SK 10/03). The Tribunal stressed (CT decision of 24 October 2001, SK 10/01) that the right to equal treatment may be considered in terms of subjective right, but is primarily a 'second degree' right ('*metaright*'), i.e., it is granted in connection with specific legal norms or other actions of public authorities, referring to specific, constitutionally defined freedoms and rights, not independent of them, as if by itself.

536. The second part of Article 32(2) prohibits discrimination in political, social or economic life 'for any reason whatsoever'. It is therefore an anti-discrimination clause most general in tone, without specifying the grounds on which discrimination could occur.

537. The Polish CT has repeatedly stressed that the principle of equality does not preclude the introduction of forms of preference for certain groups with a weaker social or economic position in order to compensate for existing inequalities (cf. decisions of the CT of 29 September 1997, K 15/97, 28 March 2000, K 27/99, 13 June 2000, K 15/99). We should particularly note the decision dated 15 July 2010 (K 63/07), concerning the lower retirement age for women, where the Tribunal expressly stated that there is a constitutional justification for the introduction of special arrangements for women compared to men, and that these arrangements are intended to ensure that women are actually treated equally – which does not have to mean that they share identical circumstances.

538. However, this kind of privilege raises certain doubts in the study of constitutional law doctrine, especially in the sphere of personal or political rights, although such privileges in the sphere of social rights are less controversial.

F. Remedies for Violations of Rights and Liberties under the Constitution

539. The Constitution contains numerous instruments for the protection and enforcement of rights and freedoms and devotes a separate subchapter just to them.

540. The guarantee of judicial pursuit of the violated rights and freedoms is the basic measure of this protection, contained in Article 77(2) of the Constitution. This guarantee is formulated in a forceful way, because the Constitution forbids the legislator to make laws that would block the judicial process of asserting the violated rights and freedoms.

541. In accordance with the principle of the highest legal force and direct applicability of the Constitution (Article 8) and the contents of the rights and freedoms provided for in the Constitution, most of the personal and political rights may serve as the basis for specific claims, i.e., they give rise to subjective rights which may be asserted before the court. Therefore, the Constitution prohibits blocking the way to pursue such claims before the courts. It is worth mentioning that the Constitution does not limit this prohibition exclusively to common courts, meaning that a party may also pursue its rights in proceedings before administrative courts, appointed to control the activities of public administration. The Constitution prohibits blocking the judicial protection against violations not only on the part of the authorities or administration, but also on the part of anyone else.

542. Another important means of protecting rights and freedoms is the right to compensation for damage caused by the illegal activity of public authority, guaranteed by Article 77(1) of the Constitution (*see* Part II., Chapter 5., §1., IV. State Liability for the Torts of Public Authorities (Article 77(1) of the Constitution)).

543. According to Article 78 of the Constitution, each party shall have the right to appeal against judgments and decisions made at first stage. Exceptions to this principle and the procedure for such appeals shall be specified by statute. Hence, this guarantee covers the right to review the verdict made in the case of the complainant. Such a review, carried out by the authority of the second instance, concerns the correctness of the course of the entire process that gave rise to the issued decision, as well as its effect; namely establishing whether factual findings were reached in compliance with the assumed procedural standards, whether the process of considering the case in the first instance and the process of adjudication were carried out properly, and whether the substantive law provisions were duly applied. This scrutiny is intended to prevent mistakes made by the first instance authority in the first place and second, possible arbitrariness or bias in the adjudication process.

544. Another measure of protection against violations of rights and freedoms is the constitutional complaint. In accordance with Article 79 of the Constitution, everyone whose constitutional freedoms or rights have been infringed shall have the right to appeal to the CT for its judgment on the conformity to the Constitution of a statute or another normative act upon which basis a court or organ of public administration has made a final decision on his freedoms or rights or on his obligations specified in the Constitution. This provision does not apply to the rights specified in Article 56, that is, the right of foreigners to be granted asylum and the status of refugee. Constitutional complaint is an important means of protecting rights and freedoms; in fact, it acts as a brake for monitoring of the legislative authority, since the object of the complaint is the conformity of a law or other normative act with the Constitution to the extent of the rights and freedoms provided for by the Constitution (*see also* Part II., Chapter 5., §2., III. The Constitutional Complaint).

545. Thus, accepting the complaint means that the Tribunal finds the provision challenged in the complaint that has given rise to an unfavourable judgment in the case incompatible with a constitutional norm guaranteeing a particular right or freedom. However, this ruling, issued on the basis of the contested provision that has been deemed unconstitutional, remains in force, since the Tribunal does not have the power to overturn the decisions of courts or other authorities. However, proceedings that conclude with a ruling that led to the complaint are resumed (in criminal proceedings) or may be requested to be resumed (in administrative and civil proceedings) if, as a result of the CT's ruling, the legal provision on which the ruling was based has lost its validity. In this way, once the proceedings are resumed, the case is re-examined without regard to the provision (part of it) that the Tribunal has declared unconstitutional.

546. According to Article 80 of the Constitution, everyone has the right to seek assistance from the Ombudsman in protecting his or her freedoms or rights violated by public authorities. Generally, the request addressed to the Ombudsman does not have to contain any formal requirements, it may be submitted in any form, and it does not have to indicate which rights or freedoms have been violated. However, the Ombudsman is not bound by the content of the request and may either take up the case or merely indicate available legal remedies; it is also possible for the Ombudsman to refer the case to the competent authority or simply not to take up the case, informing the applicant accordingly (*see also* Part II., Chapter 6., §2. The Ombudsman).

547. To conclude the discussion about measures for the protection of rights and freedoms, it should be emphasised that certain rights cannot be asserted directly on the basis of the Constitution, but only within the limits set out in statute – these are the rights set out in Article 65, paragraphs 4 and 5, Articles 66, 69, 71 and 74–76 (*see* Part IV., Chapter §4., I. Statutory Limitations of Social Rights (Article 81)).

§2. Personal Freedoms and Rights

548. Polish classification of human rights was developed in accordance with the criterion also adopted by international acts, in particular the UN Covenants on Human Rights. Hence, the Constitution divides freedoms and rights into three categories: personal, political and the third category encompassing economic, social and cultural rights.

549. Personal rights and freedoms mean those that pertain to the non-political spheres of human life, namely the sphere of personal, family and social life. Everyone is included in their scope, with the only exception being the prohibition of extradition (Article 55) which is guaranteed exclusively to Polish citizens.

I. The Legal Protection of the Life

550. Article 38 of the Constitution provides every human being with legal protection of life. The Constitution does not specify when the protection of life begins and at what point in time we can say that a human comes to life, and thus it does not definitively resolve the problem of legal protection of the conceived life. Nevertheless, there is the position of the CT in this matter, as expressed in its decision of 28 May 1997 (K 26/96), according to which the term 'human being' includes a human being in the prenatal development stage (in this case, the CT declared the provision to allow for abortion for social reasons, e.g., the mother's difficult life situation, to be incompatible with constitutional norms). Moreover, both civil law and the jurisprudence of the SC grant legal protection to the human being from the moment of conception. Since 1993 abortion has been allowed in Polish law under exceptional circumstances – namely the following three situations: (1) when the pregnancy poses a threat to the life or health of the mother, (2) prenatal examinations or other medical evidence indicate a high probability of a serious and irreversible impairment of the foetus or an incurable disease endangering its life, (3) there is a justified suspicion that the pregnancy is a result of a prohibited act (in the latter case – up to twelve weeks since the beginning of pregnancy). The Polish CT judgment issued on 22 October 2020 on the unconstitutionality of the provision of the Act allowed the termination of pregnancy for embryopathological reasons (2nd exception). The provision permitting abortion due to a defect in the foetus should expire on the date of promulgation of the Tribunal's judgment in the official publication (Journal of Laws). The judgment rose a wave of public protests lasting for many weeks. The CT judgment was finally published at the end of January 2021.

551. The legal protection of life leads to inadmissibility and lack of possibility to introduce euthanasia and assisted suicide in Poland.

552. The Polish Constitution also expressly prohibits any scientific experiments, including medical tests performed without the consent of the interested party (Article 39). This prohibition is associated with the principle of human dignity and protection of personal freedom rather than the protection of human life. The consent to an experiment must be expressed personally (with the exception of the so-called surrogate consent expressed by the guardian of a minor or an incapacitated person), voluntary and consciously, that is to say, with full awareness of the effects of the planned experiment.

II. Prohibition of Torture or Cruel, Inhuman, or Degrading Treatment or Punishment

553. The prohibition of torture and cruel, inhuman or degrading treatment or punishment, as well as the prohibition of corporal punishment are formulated in Article 40 of the Constitution. The prohibition provided for in Article 40 is absolute, that is, it is neither limited nor revoked under any circumstances.

554. Torture should be understood as a special form of inhuman treatment of another person – in Polish legal order (modelled after international standards) actions of state officials consisting of inflicting deliberately intense pain or suffering in order to intimidate, punish or exert pressure are considered torture.

555. The prohibition of degrading treatment in the context of the serving time in prison was of particular importance in the practice of the Polish justice administration system and in the reality of penitentiary – in the decision of 26 May 2008 (SK 25/07), the Tribunal stated that a provision of the Executive Penal Code, which 'in particularly justified cases' allowed for a prisoner to be placed in a cell with less than 3 square meters per prisoner, is incompatible with this prohibition. The conditions of both serving a sentence and treatment – especially compulsory one (including mentally ill persons) – are often subject to review from the point of view of this norm.

556. When it comes to implementation of this provision, there was a lot of controversy surrounding the cases of *Al Nashiri v. Poland and Huasyn (Abu Zubaydah) v. Poland* (App. Nos 28761/11 and 7511/13) settled by the ECHR in July 2014, stating that in Poland there had been a violation of Article 3 of the Convention in its procedural aspect on account of the respondent State's failure to carry out an effective investigation into the applicant's allegations of serious violations of the Convention, including torture, ill-treatment and undisclosed detention, and violation of Article 3 of the Convention in its substantive aspect, on account of the respondent State's complicity in the CIA High-Value Detainees Programme in that it enabled the United States authorities to subject the applicant to torture and ill-treatment on its territory and to transfer the applicant from its territory despite the existence of a real risk that he would be subjected to treatment contrary to Article 3.

III. Personal Inviolability and Security

557. Personal inviolability and personal freedom are guaranteed in Article 41 of the Constitution. Personal inviolability is connected, first of all, with the prohibition of violating the physical as well as mental integrity and with the prohibition of arbitrary and unlawful detention as well. As the CT stated, personal inviolability means 'freedom from arbitrary interference by public authorities in its physical, spiritual and psychological integrity' (judgment of the CT of 5 March 2013, U 2/11). In turn, personal freedom means freedom to make decisions according to one's own will (judgment of the SC of 13 March 1990, V KZP 33/89).

558. Constitutional guarantees also include the following rights of the detained person (Article 41 sections 2, 3, 4 and 5):

(a) The prohibition of deprivation of liberty or restriction of liberty, except in the cases provided for by law, under the conditions laid down therein.
(b) The right to appeal to a court for immediate decision upon the lawfulness of such deprivation.
(c) Any deprivation of liberty shall be immediately made known to the family of, or a person indicated by, the person deprived of liberty.
(d) Every detained person shall be informed, immediately and in a manner comprehensible to him, of the reasons for such detention.

(e) The person shall, within forty-eight hours of detention, be given over to a court for consideration of the case. The detained person shall be set free unless a warrant of temporary arrest issued by a court, along with specification of the charges laid, has been served on him within twenty-four hours of the time of being given over to the court's disposal.
(f) Anyone deprived of liberty shall be treated in a humane manner.
(g) Anyone who has been unlawfully deprived of liberty shall have a right to compensation.

IV. *Nulla Poena, Nullum Crimen Sine Lege*

559. The Polish Constitution explicitly provides for a set of rights and guarantees regarding criminal liability. The first is that the criminal offence must be defined by the law in force at the time it is committed, which means that the criminal law cannot have retroactive effect. Second, both constitutional and common court case law in Poland emphasises the principle according to which defining prohibited acts can only be done by way of a statute – as an act of Parliament passed under a special procedure. Third, this identification must be as precise and detailed as possible – therefore, references to sub-statutory acts are not allowed, and the use of blurred meaning phrases is examined in detail and treated restrictively. As the CT has graphically pointed out (decision of 23 June 2009, K 54/07), 'legislator cannot require a citizen to be aware of a criminal prohibition if the legislator is unable to clearly identify its scope'.

V. The Right to a Fair Trial

560. The Polish Constitution has divided the right to a fair trial into several units.

561. Article 45 of the Constitution guarantees everyone the right to a fair and public hearing by a competent, impartial and independent court. This right refers to everyone (it is not reserved for citizens only) and is included in the classic arrangement:

- the right of access to court;
- the right to a proper judicial procedure, i.e., to have it performed in accordance with the constitutional requirements for the court and the trial itself;
- the right to have the ruling given – a guarantee of a court ruling (CT ruling of 9 June 1998, K 28/97).

562. The CT added fourth element to this set, recognising that the constitutional right to a fair trial also extends to the right to the proper shaping of the system and the status of the bodies considering cases (decisions of the CT of 10 July 2000 SK 12/99 and of 24 October 2007 SK 7/06).

563. The concept of the case referred to in Article 45 is understood very broadly – it includes not only civil and criminal, but also administrative cases, as well as those that cannot be classified under these categories, as long as they require a decision by a judicial authority.

564. The guarantee that property may be forfeited only in cases specified by statute, and only by virtue of a final judgment of a court (Article 46) is also an important component of the right to a fair trial.

565. The provision of Article 42 contains an extensive set of rights and guarantees related to being held criminally liable. Its elements include the following:

- Only a person who has committed an act prohibited by statute in force at the moment of commission thereof, and which is subject to a penalty, shall be held criminally liable.
- Anyone against whom criminal proceedings have been brought shall have the right to defence at all stages of such proceedings. He may, in particular, choose counsel or avail himself – in accordance with principles specified by statute.
- Everyone shall be presumed innocent of a charge until his guilt is determined by the final judgment of a court.

566. Article 77(2) prohibits barring the recourse by any person to the courts in pursuit of claims alleging infringement of freedoms or rights (*see also* Part IV., Chapter 2., §1., IV., F. Remedies for Violations of Rights and Liberties under the Constitution).

VI. The Right to Privacy

567. The right to legal protection of everyone's private and family life is guaranteed by Article 47 of the Constitution. This provision grants legal protection of private life, family life, honour and good name, as well as the right to decide one's personal life.

568. Privacy is linked to freedom from interference into the sphere of life inaccessible to outsiders and protected against them, which covers: health, intimate life and family relations, the right to establish and maintain relations with others, ensuring the development of personality without outside interference, and sometimes, the sphere of professional life. The right to the protection of private life guaranteed by Article 47 of the Constitution is developed in other constitutional provisions which guarantee its various aspects, in particular, the right of parents to rear their children according to their own convictions (Article 48), the freedom and protection of the confidentiality of communication (Article 49) and the inviolability of housing (Article 50).

569. The right to legal protection of private life is closely correlated with the guarantees contained in Article 51 of the Constitution, i.e., the requirement of a statutory basis for an individual to be bound by the law to disclose information concerning this person, the prohibition on obtaining, collecting information about citizens other than that necessary in a democratic state and making it available by public authorities, the right of access to official documents and data collections concerning the individual and the right to demand the correction and deletion of information that is untrue, incomplete or collected in a manner contrary to statute. In the case law of the CT, the protection of private life, as provided for in Article 47, is closely linked to the autonomy in revealing information guaranteed in Article 51, which means the right to decide on disclosure of information concerning one's person to others, as well as the right to control such information if it is available to others (*see* decision of 20 November 2002, K 41/02 and of 19 February 2002, U 3/01).

VII. Freedom of Movement

570. In Article 52, Polish Constitution guarantees the freedom of movement as well as the choice of place of residence and sojourn within the territory of the RP. However, according to the Basic Law, these freedoms may be restricted by the law for a number of reasons, including the penalty of restriction of freedom, preventive measures, as well as for reasons of safeguarding certain areas (such as forests, traffic zones, border areas) or the safety and health of citizens (e.g., during a state of emergency, but also – as in spring 2020 – during a state of both epidemic threat and the epidemic).

571. The constitutional provision further prohibits the expulsion of a Polish citizen from the country and barring the return to the country. Article 52 also ensures the right to freely leave the territory of the country.

572. An interesting regulation is contained in Article 52(5), according to which anyone whose Polish origin has been confirmed in accordance with statute may settle down in Poland. This provision applies primarily to persons who have found themselves outside the territory of the RP regardless of their own decision, due to the change of state borders and the forced deportation of persons of Polish origin from the territory of the Soviet Republics – this special return procedure is included in the Repatriation Act of 9 November 2000.

VIII. Freedom of Conscience and Religion

573. The Polish Constitution devotes much space to freedom of conscience and religion and the status of churches. The latter has been standardised under constitutional principles (*see* General Introduction, §2., VII. Autonomy of Churches, Religious Impartiality of the State). Freedom of conscience and religion, on the other hand, is among personal freedoms, described in detail in Article 53 of the Constitution. This provision provides for the freedom to profess or to accept a religion by personal choice as well as to manifest such religion, either individually or collectively, publicly or privately, by worshipping, praying, participating in ceremonies, performing of rites or teaching. Freedom of religion shall also include ownership of sanctuaries and other places of worship for the satisfaction of the needs of believers as well as the right of individuals, wherever they may be, to benefit from religious services.

574. Furthermore, the Constitution provides parents with the right to ensure their children a moral and religious upbringing and teaching in accordance with their convictions (Article 53(3)).

575. The religion of a church or other legally recognised religious organisation may be taught in Polish schools.

576. The constitutional regulation also provides for two prohibitions guaranteeing full freedom of religion (as well as an atheistic worldview): the prohibition of forcing anyone to participate or not to participate in religious practices and one stating that no one must be compelled by organs of public authority to disclose their philosophy of life, religious convictions or belief.

IX. Freedom of Expression

577. Freedom of expression has been positioned in the constitutional text among the freedoms and personal rights. In turn, freedom of the press was recognised as a constitutional principle (Article 14), and thus one of the foundations of the Polish State and democratic order.

578. The Constitution (Article 54) lists the components of freedom of expression, indicating that everyone is guaranteed the freedom to voice opinions, to acquire and to disseminate information. This freedom includes all forms and content, including artistic expression, although it is mentioned separately in Article 73 (*see* Part IV., Chapter 2., §4., IV. Cultural Rights).

579. Both the Polish judicial practice and the science of the law have adopted the view – in line with the ECHR jurisprudence – that public debate allows for harsh forms of expression, which are a form of criticism, even with the use of measures of provocative nature. According to the case law of the CT, 'the constitutional powers provided for in Article 54(1) of the Constitution consist (…) of the right to engage in political debate, which is an important component of a democratic legal system. Free public debate in a democratic state is one of the most important guarantors of freedom and civic liberties', and the creation of appropriate guarantees for the exercise of freedom of expression 'is necessary with regard to both the personal and political aspects of the individual'. However, establishing the conditions for free exchange of views does not mean that all forms of expression are allowed, because the freedom in question generally excludes explicitly insulting expression (*see* CT judgment of 12 February 2015, SK 70/13, similar to the judgment of 6 July 2011,

P 12/09). Consequently, the CT declared that Article 54 covers the criminal offence of insulting the President and public officials, the same refers to the regulation on the offence of demonstrating disrespect for the Polish Nation, in which it has been stated that the regulation does not restrict freedom of expression in such a way as to make it impossible to give judgments, opinions, or even criticism of the subjects mentioned therein. In a democratic state of law, which is a common good of all citizens, public debate can and should take place in a cultured manner and free from demonstrable disregard for constitutionally important subjects. Such a requirement enforced by the legislature cannot be deemed detrimental to freedom of expression (CT judgment of 21 September 2015, K 28/13).

580. The constitutional regulation of freedom of expression also includes a ban on preventive censorship of the social media and on the licensing of the press – although the law may introduce an obligation to obtain a licence to operate a radio or television station (Article 54(2)). This regulation is closely related to Poland's past experience, since up to 1989 (formally up to 1990) there had been the system of censorship in Poland reviewing all newspapers, books, all other printed matter, as well as the performing arts.

X. The Prohibition of the Extradition of a Polish Citizen

581. In Article 52 the Constitution prohibits the expulsion of a Polish citizen from the country (*see* Part IV., Chapter 2., §2., VII. Freedom of Movement). On the other hand, Article 55 prohibits the extradition of a Polish citizen, i.e., the surrender of a Polish citizen to be tried for a committed crime or to serve a final sentence. It thus established the right of Polish citizens to have their case heard by 'their own' institution, i.e., a Polish court. Initially, the prohibition of extradition was not subject to exceptions – the provision continued to be in force until 2006. The amendment of this provision and the limitation of the prohibition of expulsion were related to the validity of the EAW Framework Decision, which became binding for Poland upon its accession to the EU. As a result, provisions concerning the surrender of Polish citizens as a result of an EAW were introduced into the Polish Code of Criminal Procedure. However, they were found to be inconsistent with the constitutional prohibition of extradition (CT judgment of 27 April 2005, P 1/05), but the Tribunal noted in its ruling that the loss of binding force would not ensure the compatibility of the legal situation with the Constitution, and postponed the loss of binding force – thus allowing time for the amendment of the relevant constitutional regulation. It was implemented in 2006 – currently Article 55 prohibits extradition, but provides for important exceptions: extradition of a Polish citizen may be granted upon a request made by a foreign State or an international judicial body if such a possibility stems from an international treaty ratified by Poland or a statute implementing a legal instrument enacted by an international organisation of which the RP is a member, provided that the act covered by a request for extradition:

(1) was committed outside the territory of the RP; and

(2) constituted an offence under the law in force in the RP or would have constituted an offence under the law in force in the RP if it had been committed within the territory of the RP, both at the time of its commitment and at the time of the making of the request;
(3) extradition request is made by an international judicial body established under an international treaty ratified by Poland, in connection with a crime of genocide, crime against humanity, war crime or a crime of aggression, covered by the jurisdiction of that body.

582. In such cases, however, extradition continues to be prohibited if it concerns a person suspected of committing a non-violent crime on political grounds or if its execution will violate human and civil liberties and rights. The admissibility of extradition shall be decided by a court.

XI. Asylum

583. According to Article 56 of the Constitution, foreigners shall have the right of asylum in the RP in accordance with principles specified by statute. Foreigners who, in the RP, seek protection from persecution, may be granted the status of a refugee in accordance with international agreements to which the RP is a party.

584. Asylum is a form of protection involving the right of the State to shelter a foreigner; such a person receives the right of permanent residence on the territory of the RP. In turn, obtaining the refugee status requires foreigners to prove that they are being persecuted on the territory of their country, and it is granted in order to provide protection against persecution. International law, in particular the Geneva Convention relating to the Status of Refugees, is of key importance for determining this status and the conditions for obtaining it.

§3. Political Freedoms and Rights

585. The freedoms and rights connected with the public sphere of human life that are guaranteed by the Constitution can be divided into those enjoyed by everyone and those reserved only for Polish citizens. The categories of freedoms and political rights that everyone enjoys regardless of their citizenship include: freedom to organise and participate in assemblies; freedom of association; and the right of everyone to submit petitions, applications and complaints. The following are reserved for Polish citizens: the right of access to public service; the right to belong to political parties; the right to obtain public information; the right to vote and participate in a referendum; the right of legislative initiative.

I. The Freedom of Peaceful Assembly

586. Article 58 of the Constitution guarantees the freedom to organise and participate in a peaceful assembly. The assembly is considered to be a temporary and simultaneous grouping of persons for an unlimited number of participants – the function of the assembly is to express a certain view (support, opposition, commemoration of an event or person). The condition for being protected under Article 58 is the peaceful nature of the assembly – which must be supervised by both the organiser and the public authorities.

587. The freedom to hold assemblies is connected with the absence of the requirement to obtain permission to do so – in Poland, the Law on Assemblies adopts a procedure of notification, i.e., notification of the intention to hold an assembly to a public (local) authority. However, apart from formally notified meetings, spontaneous gatherings are also admissible, i.e., unnotified, provided that they are held in connection with a sudden and unpredictable event related to the public sphere, the holding of which at another time would be pointless or of little importance for the public debate.

588. The task of the authorities is to ensure their safe and peaceful conduct, as well as to protect the participants of the assembly – especially in the case of counterdemonstrations – as the CT ruled, the assembly enjoys freedom regardless of whether it is widely accepted or not (CT decision of 18 January 2006, K 21/05). In its decision of 18 September 2014 (K 44/12) CT ruled that the Law on Assemblies, in the part limiting the number of participants in the assembly, was inconsistent with Article 57 in conjunction with Article 31(3) of the Polish Constitution of 1997.

589. The new Law on Assemblies was passed in 2015. According to it, the organiser of the gathering is obliged to provide notification no later than six days before the planned date of the assembly. The municipal body issues a decision to ban the assembly no later than ninety-six hours before its planned date, if:

(1) its purpose violates the freedom of peaceful assembly, it being held violates the rules of organising assemblies or the purpose of the assembly, or it being held violates criminal provisions;
(2) it being held may endanger the life or health of people or property on a significant scale;
(3) the assembly is to be held at the place and time when the regular gatherings are taking place. Thus, the statute gives priority to cyclical gatherings to choose the place and time of their organisation and formalises the mode of organisation of such gatherings. Despite many controversies that these provisions have raised, in the decision of 16 March 2017 (Kp 1/17) the CT ruled that the regulations governing the conduct of cyclical gatherings are consistent with the constitutional principles of equality and the rule of law, as well as freedom of association.

590. No gatherings were allowed in the spring of 2020 because of the COVID-19 pandemic. This ban was constitutionally controversial because it was introduced in the regulation of the Minister of Health and then in the government regulation without the introduction of a constitutionally sanctioned state of emergency.

II. The Freedom of Association

591. Freedom of association and freedom of creation and functioning of political parties are elevated to the rank of political principles in Articles 11 and 12 of the Constitution (*see* General Introduction, §2., V. National Sovereignty, Forms of Democracy).

592. The freedom of association is guaranteed as an individual right in Article 58. The Constitution does not prejudge the form of associations, nor does it provide for any formal conditions for their formation or existence, but allows for regulating the types of associations subject to judicial registration and supervision by way of statute.

593. The Constitution also provides for the prohibition of associations, whose purpose or activity is contrary to the Constitution or the law, the prohibition of an association must always be decided upon by the court. As far as political parties are concerned, only the CT may decide on the incompatibility of their activities or objectives with the Constitution (Article 188(4)).

594. Trade unions and employers' organisations are also particularly standardised forms of association as indicated by the Constitution. According to Article 59, everyone has the right to associate in trade unions, socio-occupational organisations of farmers' and employers' organisations. Trade unions and employers and their organisations have the right to bargain, particularly for the purpose of resolving collective disputes, and to conclude collective labour agreements and other arrangements. Additionally, trade unions have the right to organise workers' strikes or other forms of protest subject to limitations specified by statute. For protection of the public interest, statutes may limit or forbid the conduct of strikes by specified categories of employees or in specific fields.

III. The Right of Access to the Public Service

595. According to Article 60 of the Constitution, Polish citizens enjoying full public rights shall have the right of access to the public service based on the principle of equality. Public service is understood as a specific type of activity related to not only the exercise of public authority but also the organisational structure related to employment and special service relationship, in order to perform the tasks entrusted by the State.

596. Guaranteeing access to the service on equal terms means that all requirements – formal and material – must be precisely defined and objectified by law. The same conditions apply to the mode and conditions of selection of candidates meeting the initial requirements.

IV. The Right to Obtain Public Information

597. Article 61 of the Constitution guarantees every citizen the right to obtain information on the activities of organs of public authority as well as persons discharging public functions. The provision also indicates that this right also includes receipt of information on the activities of self-governing economic or professional organs and other persons or organisational units relating to the field in which they perform the duties of public authorities and manage communal assets or state property.

598. In accordance with the constitutional standard, the right to obtain information shall ensure access to documents and entry to sittings of collective organs of public authority formed by universal elections, with the opportunity to make sound and visual recordings (Article 61(2)).

599. The constitutional right of access to public information may be limited only because of the protection of the freedom and rights of other persons and economic entities as well as the protection of public order, security or an important economic interest of the State, as specified in the laws; these are therefore other legitimate aims than those provided for in Article 31(3) of the Constitution; the extension of the catalogue to include an important economic interest of the State is particularly noteworthy.

600. The mode of providing information is regulated primarily by the Act on Access to Public Information. The collision of the right of access and the protection of privacy of persons whose data appear in the content of public documents is highly controversial – there is rich jurisprudence of administrative courts which control the mode and correctness of decisions providing public information and refusing to provide it.

V. The Right to Vote

601. Pursuant to Article 62 of the Constitution, a Polish citizen if, no later than on the day of vote, he/she has attained 18 years of age, shall have the right to participate in a referendum and the right to vote for the President of the RP as well as representatives to the Sejm and the Senate and organs of local government.

602. The right to vote is a fundamental political right and an individual aspect of the principle of universality of elections (*see* Part II., Chapter 2., §1., II., D. Voters)

603. The Constitution makes the right to vote depending on two conditions: nationality and age. It should be added, however, that the legislator has extended the right to participate in local self-government elections to include EU citizens living in the territory of the bodies for which the elections are held. Despite the controversy it raised, this provision was found to be consistent with the constitutional regulation by the CT (CT decision of 11 May 2005, K 18/04).

604. The constitutional provision also indicates the permissible limitations of the electoral law. These are:

(1) incapacitation – i.e., a court decision concerning the declaration of incapacity to direct one's actions – against persons who are mentally ill, handicapped or suffering from other mental disorders;
(2) deprivation of public rights – this is a criminal measure, used to punish a crime committed 'as a result of motivation deserving special condemnation' for at least three years of imprisonment;
(3) disenfranchisement – this is the punishment that the TS can apply when deciding on the constitutional responsibility of high officials (*see* Part II., Chapter 5., §3., Th*e* Tribunal of State).

605. It is worth noting that only the court or the TS is entitled to disenfranchisement (deprive a right to vote) under these conditions.

606. Further limitations apply to the right to stand as a candidate (passive electoral right). According to Article 99(3), no person sentenced to imprisonment by a final judgment for an intentional indictable offence may be elected to the Sejm or the Senate. This rule also applies to the election of the President (Article 127(3)).

VI. The Right to Petition

607. According to Article 63 of the Constitution, everyone has the right to submit petitions, proposals and complaints in the public interest, in his own interest or in the interests of another person – with his consent – to organs of public authority, as well as to organisations and social institutions in connection with the performance of their prescribed duties within the field of public administration. The procedures for considering petitions, proposals and complaints shall be specified by statute.

608. Petitions, complaints and applications may be submitted to state bodies, e.g., the Sejm, the President of the RP, the Minister, as well as to local government bodies and social organisations and institutions in connection with their public administration tasks.

609. Any legal acts of the competent bodies or employee, decisions, other legal actions or lack thereof may serve as the subject of a petition (motion). The procedure of examining petitions, applications and complaints was initially defined by the Code of Administrative Procedure, and from 2014 the Petitions Act.

§4. ECONOMIC, SOCIAL AND CULTURAL FREEDOMS AND RIGHTS

I. Statutory Limitations of Social Rights (Article 81)

610. The catalogue of economic, social and cultural freedoms and rights has raised serious controversies and concerns about the adoption of workable solutions that can be applied in practice and assessed by the CT evaluated in light of prevailing market economy. The adopted catalogue is therefore the result of a trade-off. The legislature also assumed that some of these rights enjoy limited protection. These are the rights specified in the Articles: 65 sections 4 and 5 (setting a minimum level of remuneration and the policy of public authorities aimed at full employment), 66 (the right to safe and hygienic working conditions, days free from work and paid annual holidays), 69 (guarantee of public authorities' aid for the disabled), 71 (assistance for families and the requirement to consider family welfare in social and economic policy, assistance to mothers), 74 (an obligation imposed on public authorities to pursue policies that ensure environmental safety and nature protection as well as the right to information on the quality of such protection), 75 (an obligation imposed on public authorities to pursue policies conducive to satisfying the housing needs of citizens), and 76 (an obligation imposed on public authorities to protect consumers, customers and tenants from actions that threaten them).

611. These rights may be asserted under Article 81 of the Constitution subject to limitations specified by statute, which means that when invoking these rights, it is essential to indicate their statutory basis, not the constitutional one.

612. The scope of these rights, the degree of their protection and their performance are to be determined by statutes, not by the Constitution, which in fact declares only a certain policy to be implemented in this regard by public authorities. The degree of protection and guarantee of these rights by the Constitution essentially demonstrates a dimension of a certain course of action pursued by public authorities, but does not give rise to subjective rights for individuals.

II. Economic Rights

613. The catalogue of economic, social and cultural rights and freedoms begins with the right to property, other property rights and inheritance. Protection of ownership and the right of succession, as well as the admissibility of expropriation for public purposes only and with just compensation, was raised to the rank of a principle by the Polish legislator (Article 21 of the Constitution). As provided for in

Article 64, everyone has the right to ownership, other property rights and the right of succession. Ownership, other property rights and the right of succession are subject to equal legal protection for everyone. Furthermore, Article 64 guarantees that the ownership may be limited only by law and only to the extent that it does not violate the essence of the property right. There is a correlation with the content of this standard with the guarantee specified in Article 46, which stipulates that the forfeiture of property may be adjudicated only by courts.

614. In addition to the principle of protecting property, the first chapter of the Constitution also provides for the principle of freedom of economic activity (Article 22). This principle, together with the principle of equal protection of property, constituting the basis of the economic system of the RP, is the right of everyone who is subject to the jurisdiction of the Polish State. Restriction of the freedom of economic activity is allowed only by way of statute and only for reasons of important public interest.

615. The Constitution also grants everyone the freedom to choose and exercise their profession and to choose their place of work. The obligation to work can only be imposed by law, and the permanent employment of minors under 16 is prohibited.

III. Social Rights

616. The right to social security in case of inability to work due to illness or disability and after reaching retirement age is reserved exclusively for citizens, as is the right to social security for citizens who remain unemployed involuntarily and have no means of subsistence. At the same time, the Constitution states that the scope and forms of social security are defined by statute.

617. The Constitution guarantees everyone the right to healthcare. It also obliges public authorities to ensure that citizens, regardless of their financial situation, have equal access to medical services financed from public funds. The public authorities are also responsible for providing proper healthcare to children, pregnant women, the disabled and the elderly, as well as for combating epidemic diseases and preventing the negative effects of environmental degradation on health.

618. The RP also ensures protection of children's rights. Everyone has the right to demand that public authorities protect children from violence, cruelty, exploitation and demoralisation. Furthermore, a child deprived of parental care has the right to be cared for and assisted by public authorities, and in the course of determining the rights of the child, public authorities and persons responsible for the child are obliged to listen to and, as far as possible, take into account the opinion of the child. The Constitution also provides for the appointment of an Ombudsman for Children, leaving it to the statute to regulate the mode of appointment and its competencies.

IV. Cultural Rights

619. Cultural rights guaranteed by the Polish Constitution include rights related to education and artistic culture.

620. According to Article 70 of the Constitution everyone has the right to education; it is obligatory in Poland until the age of 18. The Constitution also guarantees that education in public schools is free of charge, while a statute may allow certain educational services to be provided by public schools of higher education for a fee. The right to education also includes the right of parents to choose schools other than public ones for their children along with the right of citizens and institutions to establish primary, secondary and higher schools and educational development institutions.

621. However, it is the public authorities' responsibility to ensure that citizens have universal and equal access to education, in particular to create and support the systems of individual financial and organisational aid for pupils and students to facilitate this. The Constitution also guarantees the autonomy of higher education institutions, which is to be the guarantee of free development of scientific and didactic activity, determined by the direction followed by the university.

622. The Constitution also guarantees everyone the freedom of artistic creation, scientific research, the announcement of its results, the freedom to teach, as well as to make use of cultural resources.

623. The freedom of artistic creation means the liberty to undertake any artistic activity, also in terms of its form and manner (method) of performance, as well as the freedom to disseminate its output. The possibility of freely announcing the output of artistic activity is an indispensable premise for its performance, because art is a kind of human activity whose features take final shape only in the contact between the work and the recipient. In this sense, the contact with the recipient of a work of art is an essential, final element of the creative process and freedom of artistic activity.

§5. Obligations of Citizens under the Polish Constitution

624. The constitutional regulation of freedom and rights also regulates the duties of a human being and a citizen. An obligation shall be understood as an injunction or prohibition of a certain conduct addressed to an individual as defined by legal norms. A civic obligation, on the other hand, is such an order or prohibition, the establishment of which results from the nationality of the obliged person.

625. Obligations pertain to the necessity of ensuring the interests of other persons and consist in taking or abandoning certain actions which affect the situation of persons or communities (also effects of such actions). Social life gives rise to numerous relationships in which the obligations of the individual towards others arise, with only some of them being elevated by the constitutional order to the rank of the obligations listed in the Constitution, and indicates that these obligations are of considerable gravity.

626. The constitutional obligations incumbent on all those who fall under the jurisdiction of the Polish Republic are:

(1) obligation to observe the law of the RP;
(2) obligation to bear public burdens and benefits, including taxes, as defined by statute; it ought to be mentioned that the regulation contained in Article 84 concerning this obligation also plays the role of a guarantee, as it provides that the imposition of public burdens may only take place by way of statute;
(3) obligation to protect the state of the environment, which is connected with the statutory way of enforcement of responsibility for the degradation of the environment caused by an individual, provided for in Article 86.

627. Polish citizens are also obliged to be loyal to the RP and to care for the common good. This duty is closely connected with the next one – the duty to defend the homeland and the resulting duty of military service provided for in Article 85 of the Constitution. At the same time, the Constitution provides for the possibility of performing substitute service for those citizens who are not allowed to undertake military service because of religious beliefs or moral principles. Furthermore, this element is potentially significant, since the duty of basic service is currently suspended in Poland and the Armed Forces have been professionalised.

Part V. Extraordinary Measures: Martial Law, a State of Emergency or a State of Natural Disaster

§1. Introducing of Extraordinary Measures

628. The Polish Constitution states that extraordinary measures may be introduced in situations of particular danger. Depending on threat, martial law, a state of emergency or a state of natural disaster may be applied. The appropriate extraordinary measure can be introduced if ordinary constitutional measures are inadequate.

629. According to Article 228 extraordinary measures may be introduced only by regulation, issued upon the basis of statute. The regulation requires promulgation in order to be valid.

630. There are three statutes that separately regulate every extraordinary measure in details: martial law, state of emergency and state of natural disaster. The statutes provide the principles for activity by organs of public authority as well as the degree to which the freedoms and rights of persons and citizens may be subject to limitation for the duration of a period requiring any extraordinary measures. The statutes specify the principles, scope and manner of compensating for loss of property resulting from limitation of the freedoms and rights of persons and citizens during a period requiring introduction of extraordinary measures.

631. The state of martial law shall be declared in the case of external threats to the State, acts of armed aggression against the territory of the RP or when an obligation of common defence against aggression arises by virtue of an international agreement. Martial law is declared by the President of the Republic on request of the Council of Ministers, on the part of or upon the whole territory of the State.

632. The state of emergency shall be introduced in the case of threats to the constitutional order of the State, security of the citizenry or public order. Such state is introduced by the President of the Republic on request of the Council of Ministers for a definite period no longer than ninety days, in a part of or upon the whole territory of the State. Extension of the state of emergency may be made once only for a period no longer than sixty days and with the consent of the Sejm.

633. The President of the Republic shall submit the regulation on the introduction of martial law or a state of emergency to the Sejm within forty-eight hours of signing such regulation. The Sejm shall immediately consider the regulation of the President. The Sejm, by the absolute majority of votes taken in the presence of at least half the statutory number of Deputies, may annul the regulation of the President.

634. The third extraordinary measure may be introduced by the Council of Ministers in order to prevent or remove the consequences of a natural catastrophe or a technological accident exhibiting characteristics of a natural disaster. A state of natural disaster may be introduced for a definite period no longer than thirty days, on the part of or upon the whole territory of the State. Extension of the state of natural disaster may be made following the consent of the Sejm.

635. Apart from the chapter on states of emergency, the Constitution also provides for the state of war. In accordance with Article 116 the Sejm shall declare in the name of the RP the state of war and the conclusion of peace. The Sejm may adopt a resolution on the state of war only in the event of armed aggression against the territory of the RP or when an obligation of common defence against aggression arises by virtue of international agreements. If the Sejm cannot assemble for a sitting, the President of the Republic may declare the state of war. This state is similar to martial law, but it is assumed that the state of war has more of an international dimension while martial law regulates the organisation and operation of the state in internal relations.

636. Due to the SARS-CoV-2 virus, which has caused COVID-19 pandemic, the law on this extraordinary situation was also passed on 2 March 2020 (Act of 2 March 2020 on specific solutions related to the preventing, counteracting and combating COVID-19, other infectious diseases and crisis situations caused by them, Journal of Laws, item 374). In relation to this act, the state of epidemic threat was introduced first (13 March 2020), and then the state of epidemics (20 March 2020). This law regulates the actions of state authorities and the restriction of individual rights in a manner similar to that provided for in the case of a natural disaster. Nevertheless, it was not decided to introduce the state of natural disaster despite the undertaking of extraordinary constitutional measures (the Act of 2 March 2020 allows, for example, to change the content of the acts by the ordinance of the Minister – e.g., Article 28 with regard to the education law and its temporary validity – 180 days after its entry into force). The discussion on the introduction of the aforementioned states focused on the supplementary elections in communes held on 22 March 2020 and the presidential election scheduled for 10 May 2020. Ultimately, local government by-elections were held, but the presidential election was not held on the originally set date. They were held on 28 June 2020 and 12 July 2020 (second round).

637. This practice reveals that the introduction of the state of emergency is not welcomed, especially in the context of limiting or delaying the exercise of electoral rights (presidential plane crash and flooding in 2010, COVID-19 pandemic in 2020) as well as the painful memories of martial law introduced in 1981 to stifle the democratic opposition.

§2. Functioning of Legislative and Executive

638. The Constitution does not devote much space to the activities of state authorities during states of emergency, leaving the choice of measures to the legislator. However, the legislator should adhere to the principles provided for in the Constitution. Above all, it shall be the principle of proportionality, according to which actions undertaken as a result of the introduction of any extraordinary measure shall be proportionate to the degree of threat and shall be intended to achieve the swiftest restoration of conditions allowing for the normal functioning of the State. The Constitution limits the possibility for the legislator to act during the state of emergency. During a period of introduction of extraordinary measures, the following shall not be subject to change: the Constitution, the Acts on Elections to the Sejm, the Senate and organs of local government, the Act on Elections to the Presidency, as well as statutes on extraordinary measures. In practice, what proves to be the most problematic is that during a period of extraordinary measures, as well as within the period of ninety days following its termination, the term of office of the Sejm may not be shortened, nor may a nationwide referendum, nor elections to the Sejm, Senate, organs of local government nor elections for the Presidency be held, and the term of office of such organs shall be appropriately prolonged. Elections to organs of local government shall be possible only in those places where the extraordinary measures have not been introduced.

639. In addition to these restrictions, it is assumed that during states of emergency the state bodies will operate in a normal way and under normal structures. Only for a time of war (a state of affairs that may correspond to the state of war or martial law) the President of the Republic shall appoint the Commander-in-Chief of the Armed Forces on request of the Prime Minister. He/she may dismiss the Commander-in-Chief of the Armed Forces in accordance with the same procedure. Also during a time of war, extraordinary courts or special procedures may be established. Additionally, during a period of martial law, whenever, the Sejm is unable to assemble for a sitting, the President shall, on application from the Council of Ministers, issue regulations having the force of statute. Such regulations must be approved by the Sejm at its next sitting. However, the COVID-19 pandemic in 2020 indicated that the problem of the Sejm convening for a session and the legislature's ability to make laws may also occur in other states of emergency and may be difficult to overcome under the constitutional regulation, as it does not provide any legal solutions in this respect. An example of this is the remote holding of both the Sejm and the Senate sittings and voting during the COVID-19 pandemic.

§3. Limitations of Exercising Rights and Liberties

640. In Article 233, the Constitution provides for two categories of rights in relation to their limitation in states of emergency. The first category includes so-called non-derogable rights. The statute specifying the scope of limitation of the freedoms and rights of persons and citizens in times of martial law and states of emergency shall not limit the freedoms and rights specified in Article 30 (the dignity of the person), Articles 34 and 36 (citizenship), Article 38 (protection of life), Article 39, Articles 40 and 41, paragraph 4 (humane treatment), Article 42 (ascription of criminal responsibility), Article 45 (access to a court), Article 47 (personal rights), Article 53 (conscience and religion), Article 63 (petitions), as well as Articles 48 and 72 (family and children).

641. The other limitation concerns those rights that may be limited. The statute specifying the scope of limitations of the freedoms and rights of persons and citizens during states of natural disasters may limit the freedoms and rights specified in Article 22 (freedom of economic activity), Article 41, sections 1, 3 and 5 (personal freedom), Article 50 (inviolability of the home), Article 52(1) (freedom of movement and sojourn on the territory of the RP), Article 59(3) (the right to strike), Article 64 (the right of ownership), Article 65(1) (freedom to work), Article 66(1) (the right to safe and hygienic conditions of work), as well as Article 66(2) (the right to rest).

642. The anti-discrimination clause in the context of emergencies is less stringent. Limitation of the freedoms and rights of persons and citizens only by reason of race, gender, language, faith or lack of it, social origin, ancestry or property shall be prohibited. Nevertheless, it has not yet been applied in practice.

Selected Bibliography

Banaszak Bogusław (ed.), *Constitutional Law in Poland*. The Hague, London, New York: Kluwer Law International, 2012.

Banaszak Bogusław, 'Poland: Local Government in Poland: Towards Consolidation?'. In *Local Government in Europe. The 'Fourth Level' in the EU Multilayered System of Governance*, edited by Panara Carlo & Varney Michael R. Routledge, London and New York 2013.

Banaszak Bogusław, 'The Model of Executive Power in Poland: Outline of Political Evolution'. *European Public Law* 15 (2009): 171–182.

Bernatt Marcin, 'Ziółkowski Michał, Statutory Anti-Constitutionalism'. *Washington International Law Journal* 28 (2019): 487.

Bień-Kacała Agnieszka, et al. (eds.), *Liberal Constitutionalism – Between Individual and Collective Interests*. Toruń: Wydział Prawa I Administracji UMK, 2017.

Bień-Kacała Agnieszka, Tarnowska Anna & Włoch Wojciech, 'The Nation, Delegation, and Constitutional Change in Poland'. *Hungarian Journal of Legal Studies* 59 (2018): 355–377.

Drinóczi Tímea & Bień-Kacała Agnieszka (eds.), *Rule of Law, Common Values, and Illiberal Constitutionalism. Poland and Hungary Within the European Union*. London and New York: Routledge, 2020.

Drinóczi Tímea & Bień-Kacała Agnieszka. 'Illiberal Constitutionalism: The Case of Hungary and Poland'. *German Law Journal* 20 (2019): 1140–1166.

Goetz Klaus H. & Zubek Radosław, 'Government, Parliament and Law-Making in Poland'. *Journal of Legislative Studies* 13 (2007): 517–538.

Granat Mirosław & Katarzyna Granat, *The Constitution of Poland. A Contextual Analysis*. Oxford, London, New York, New Delhi, Sydney: Hart Publishing, 2019.

Jaremba Urszula, *National Judges as EU Law Judges: The Polish Civil Law System* (Nijhoff Studies in European Union Law). Brill – Nijhoff 2013.

Kustra Aleksandra, 'Reading the Tea Leaves: The Polish Constitutional Tribunal and the Preliminary Ruling Procedure'. *German Law Journal* 16 (2015): 1543–1568.

Łozowski Adam, 'Accession Treaty: Polish Constitutional Tribunal – Conformity of the Accession Treaty with the Polish Constitution. Decision of 11 May 2005'. *European Constitutional Review* 3 (2007): 148–162.

Machnikowska Anna (eds.), *The Legitimation of Judicial Power*. Gdańsk: Gdańsk University Press, 2017.

Selected Bibliography

Młynarska-Sobaczewska Anna, 'Polish Constitutional Crisis: Political Dispute of Falling Kelsenian Dogma of Constitutional Review'. *European Public Law* 23, no. 3 (2017): 489–506.

Młynarska-Sobaczewska Anna, 'Recent Polish Public Reforms'. *European Public Law* 24, no. 2 (2018): 195–212.

Nußberger Angelika, 'Poland: The Constitutional Tribunal on the implementation of the European Arrest Warrant'. *International Journal of Constitutional Law* 6 (2008): 162–170.

Sadurski Wojciech, How Democracy Dies (in Poland): A Case Study of Anti-Constitutional Populist Backsliding, Legal Studies Research Paper No. 18/01, http://ssrn.com/abstract=3103491.

Sadurski Wojciech, *Polish Constitutional Breakdown*. Oxford: Oxford University Press, 2019.

Sadurski Wojciech, *Rights Before Courts: A Study of Constitutional Courts in Postcommunist States of Central and Eastern Europe*, Springer 2013.

Scheppele Kim Lane, 'A Comparative View of the Chief Justice Role'. *University of Pennsylvania Law Review* 154 (2005–2006).

Śledzińska-Simon Anna, 'Constitutional Identity in 3D: A Model of Individual, Relational, and Collective Self and Its Application in Poland'. *International Journal of Constitutional Law* 13 (2015): 124–155.

Śledzińska-Simon Anna, 'The Rise and Fall of Judicial Self-Government in Poland: On Judicial Reform Reversing Democratic Transition'. *German Law Journal* 7 (2018): 1839–1869.

Wróblewski Mirosław, 'The Legal Value and Implementation of the Charter of Fundamental Rights in Poland'. In *Making the Charter of Fundamental Rights a Living Instrument*, edited by Palmisano Giuseppe. Brill: Nijhoff, 2015.

Wyrzykowski Mirosław & Cieleń Agnieszka. 'Presidential Elements in Government Poland – Semi-presidentialism or 'Rationalised Parliamentarianism'? *European Constitutional Law Review* 2 (2006): 253–267.

Zubik Marek (ed.), *Human Rights in Contemporary World.* Warszawa: Wydawnictwo Sejmowe, 2017.

Index

The numbers here refer to paragraph numbers.

Index

www.ingramcontent.com/pod-product-compliance
Lightning Source LLC
Chambersburg PA
CBHW071342230926
51846CB00002B/418
9789403533001